SECRET SWANAGE AND AROUND

Andrew Jackson

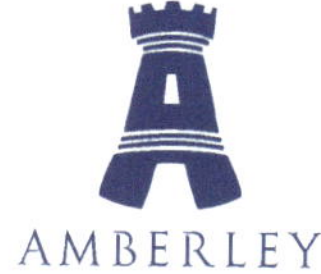

First published 2024

Amberley Publishing
The Hill, Stroud
Gloucestershire, GL5 4EP

www.amberley-books.com

ISBN 978 1 3981 1664 1 (print)
ISBN 978 1 3981 1665 8 (ebook)

British Library Cataloguing in Publication Data.
A catalogue record for this book is available from the
British Library.

Origination by Amberley Publishing.
Printed in Great Britain.

Appointed GPSR EU Representative: Easy Access
System Europe Oü, 16879218
Address: Mustamäe tee 50, 10621, Tallinn, Estonia
Contact Details: gpsr.requests@easproject.com, +358
40 500 3575

Contents

Introduction

Today the town of Swanage is a delightful Victorian seaside resort and tourist haven. However, the roots of the town were originally with fishing, before the quarrying industry in the area became paramount in the eighteenth and nineteenth centuries and Swanage evolved into an important port, from where the Purbeck stone and marble from the numerous quarries in the vicinity were transported onwards to destinations all over the world.

John Mowlem provided the catalyst for the town's further development, when he created a successful building business in London, into which he later welcomed his nephew, George Burt, as a partner. The business involved importing stone into London for various building projects and much of the stone came from the Purbeck quarries including Tilly Whim, where Mowlem toiled in his youth with his family.

Between them, Mowlem and Burt were responsible for many of the town's buildings and amenities. They had a penchant for old buildings and monuments that were no longer wanted in London and utilised the stone ships returning from the capital to bring the stone from these old buildings to Swanage. This process also served a dual purpose, as the returning stone provided ballast to prevent the ships from overturning. The buildings were then reassembled in Swanage and these former London monuments still adorn the town today.

The company won many prestigious contracts in London, including the repaving of Blackfriars Bridge, London Bridge and the Strand. They also rebuilt both Billingsgate and Smithfield markets and continued to go from strength to strength. The business expanded over many years and became the world renowned Mowlem Construction Company, which was only relatively recently acquired by Carillion in 2006.

In their respective retirements, which were forty-two years apart, both men returned to their native Swanage and became wealthy philanthropists, who sank money into worthy projects that greatly benefitted the town.

Another important figure in the development of Swanage was Dorset MP William Morton-Pitt, who had seen the town of Weymouth transform as a result of the patronage of George III (r. 1760–1820) and his strange pastime of sea bathing. Morton-Pitt was convinced that he could replicate that same success with Swanage and turn the town into a fashionable health and sea bathing resort, to rival its Dorset neighbour. Accordingly in the 1820s, Pitt initiated the first major hotel in Swanage, the Manor House Hotel, which was later renamed the Royal Victoria Hotel following a visit by the then Princess Victoria.

However, it wasn't until 1885 when George Burt instigated the opening of the railway line and, simultaneously, the building of the second new pier, for the use of pleasure steamers, that Swanage really started to take off as a tourist destination.

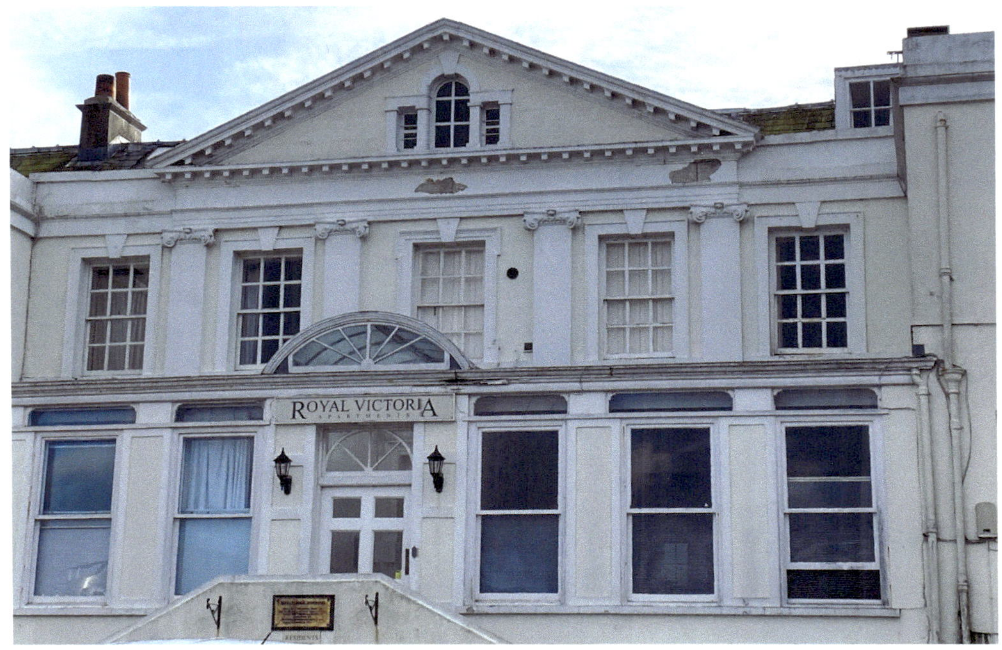

The Royal Victoria Apartments were formerly the Royal Victoria Hotel and before that the Manor House Hotel, which held the distinction of being the first hotel in Swanage.

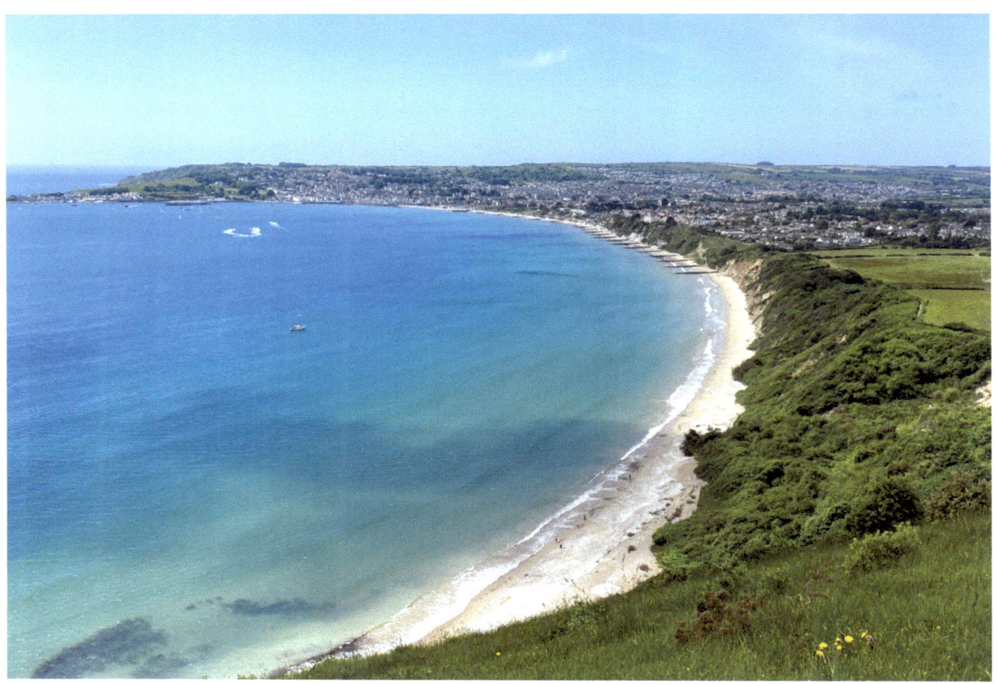

Swanage Bay.

1. The Quarrying Industry in Swanage and the Purbecks

Situated between Old Harry and Durlston Head, Swanage falls within the youngest Cretaceous section of the Jurassic Coast, where the rocks are chalk and were formed about 65 million years ago.

However, at Durlston head extending to St Aldhelm's Head, the geological situation changes and the rocks comprise of older rocks in the form of Portland limestone, which were formed in the Jurassic period between 145 million years to 206 million years ago when the British Isles were where southern Spain and northern Africa are now. During this period, the environment fluctuated over the years from tropical seas, swamps, forests and rivers. Allied to this, the subsequent collisions of tectonic plates and the resultant tilting and folding of rock layers have added to the complex geological conundrum that exists in this part of the Purbecks.

Portland limestone was deposited during the period of shallow tropical seas and of course this rock is most successfully quarried on the Isle of Portland. However sitting above the Portland limestone are the younger Purbeck Beds, which are a series of layers of limestones and clays, which were deposited about 145 to 135 million years ago and were formed during the period when the land was covered by swamps as opposed to tropical seas.

Purbeck marble is another type of Purbeck stone which formed during the early Cretaceous period of 145 to 100 million years ago. It was formed from the compacted shells of the millions of dead viviparous shells that thrived, when the area was covered in warm shallow seas as opposed to swamps. The limestone that formed in this way differs from ordinary limestone in that it can be polished to a high sheen and worked in the same way as true marble.

Limestone quarrying has long been important to Swanage and it was Purbeck marble that was the first stone to be quarried in any great quantities. The Romans were the first to appreciate the decorative appeal of the stone and they were also the first to realise that it could be polished to a lustrous sheen of blue, grey, green or red.

After the Romans left the area, quarrying declined, but the practice was revived in the twelfth century as the marble was used for internal features in prominent ecclesiastical buildings. As a result, Purbeck marble adorns many local churches, including St James's Church, Kingston, and the font at the Church of St Edward the Martyr in Corfe Castle. There are also Purbeck marble effigies and coffins to be seen in Lady St Mary's Church, Wareham. Furthermore, it has been used in several cathedrals including, Salisbury, Lincoln, Durham, Worcester and even Westminster Abbey. It is often to be seen on elaborate tombs and on ledger slabs, which are floor slabs covering burial sites, as well as in finely polished internal columns. Purbeck marble was and still is extracted in vast quantities and is mined all over the Purbecks from Worbarrow Tout in the west to Peveril Point in the east.

A community of skilled stonemasons grew up in the settlement that developed around Corfe Castle in the twelfth to the fifteenth century, as the village became a flourishing centre for the Purbeck marble trade. The craftsmen created wonderful Purbeck marble effigies and provided services to the castle, as they set up workshops and yards in what is now West Street.

The stone was transported from the surrounding quarries by donkeys pulling heavily laden carts across Corfe Common. The masons then applied their magic, before the donkeys were mobilised again to drag the finished products across Rempstone Heath to Ower Quay and other ports on Poole Harbour, from where the stone figures and effigies were destined for churches and ecclesiastical buildings throughout the land. However, after the siege of Corfe Castle and its subsequent destruction in 1646, the masonry industry in West Street went into decline.

One old tradition relating to the old Corfe Castle masonry industry is still upheld every year on Shrove Tuesday and has been in existence since the custom was instigated in 1651, by the Ancient Order of Purbeck Marblers and Stonecutters. This tradesman's guild

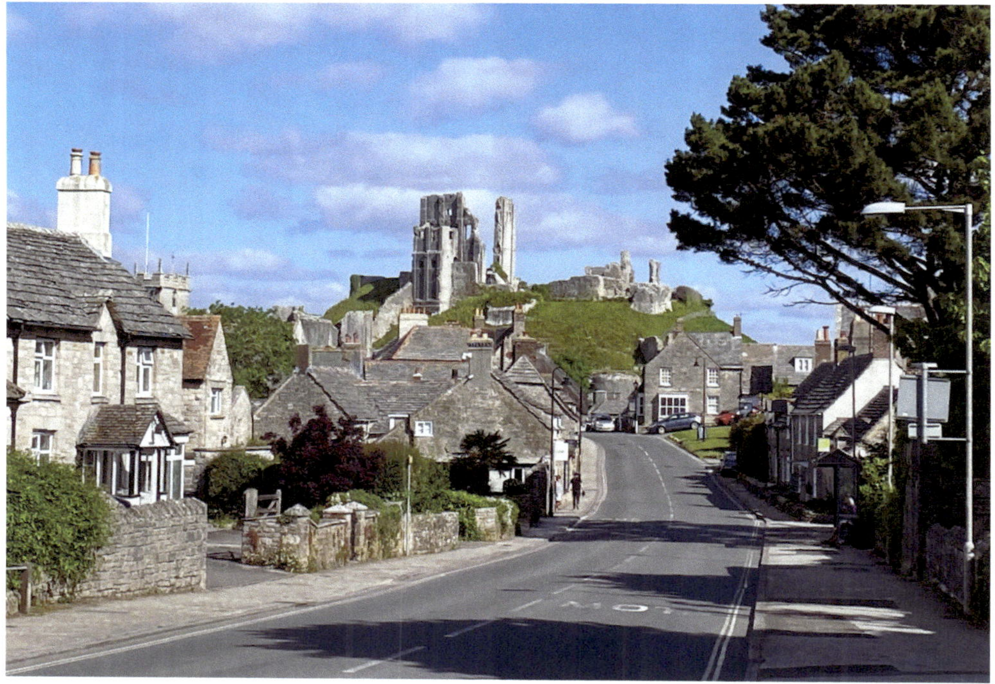

Some houses in the village of Corfe Castle still possess the original stone from when the castle was blown up in 1646, whilst many of the other older houses in the village are built of stone quarried locally and brought in by horse and cart.

was believed to have been established at the time of Henry VIII (r. 1509–1547) and is also believed to be the first Guild of Craftsman in England.

Proceedings get underway when the apprentices gather in the Fox Inn, West Street, and partake of a few beers, whilst waiting until noon for the toll of the bell of the Church of St Edward the Martyr, situated opposite, to summon them to attend the annual session of the order at the Town Hall. At the meeting, a vote is taken on whether to accept the apprentices into the order and thus to allow them to become freemen of their trade.

However, that is not the end of the proceedings as the charter further stipulates that, 'Every man of the company, the Shrove Tuesday after his marriage, shall pay rent unto the wardens for the benefit of this company, twelve pence and the last married man is to bring a football, which shall be kicked from Corfe Castle to Ower Quay, in order to preserve the marbler's right of way and upon reaching Ower Farm; the tenant of the said farm (who for this purpose represents the Lord of the Manor), shall be presented with a pound of peppercorns as rent for use of the right of way to the quay and to preserve the company's right to ship stone from that quay'.

It is an arduous trek of 12 miles from Corfe Castle to Ower Quay and no doubt kicking a football all the way makes the trek even more demanding. This probably explains why nowadays the Marblers, who are likely to be in a severely weakened state due to the amount of beer consumed up to this point, kick the ball (known as the peppercorn ball) around the boundaries of Corfe in order to preserve the old right of way and then

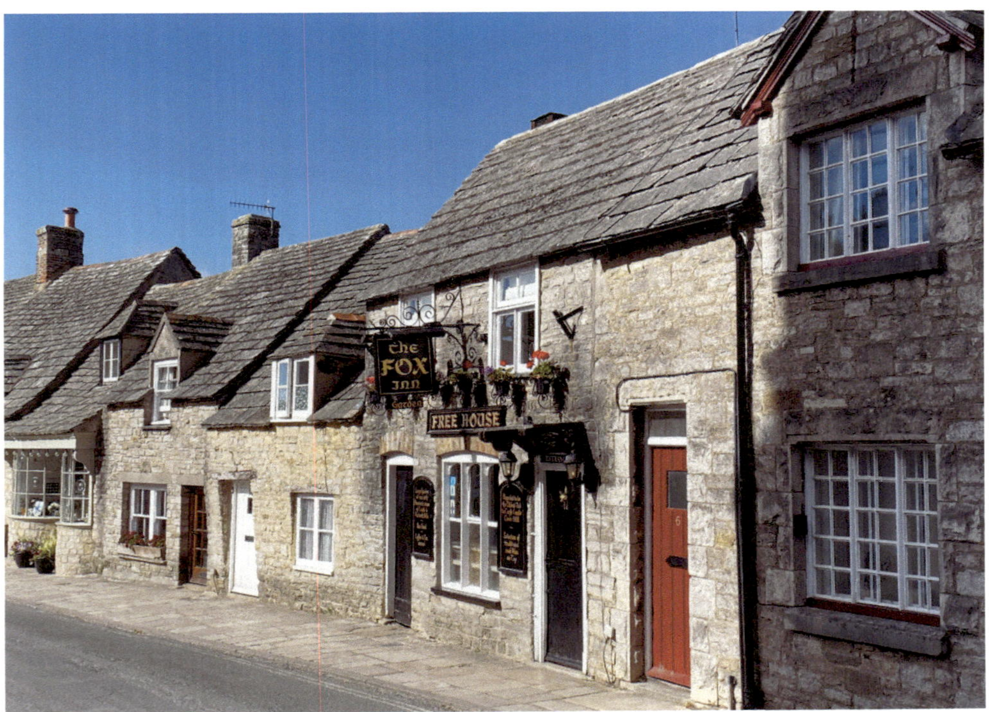

The Fox – Corfe Castle.

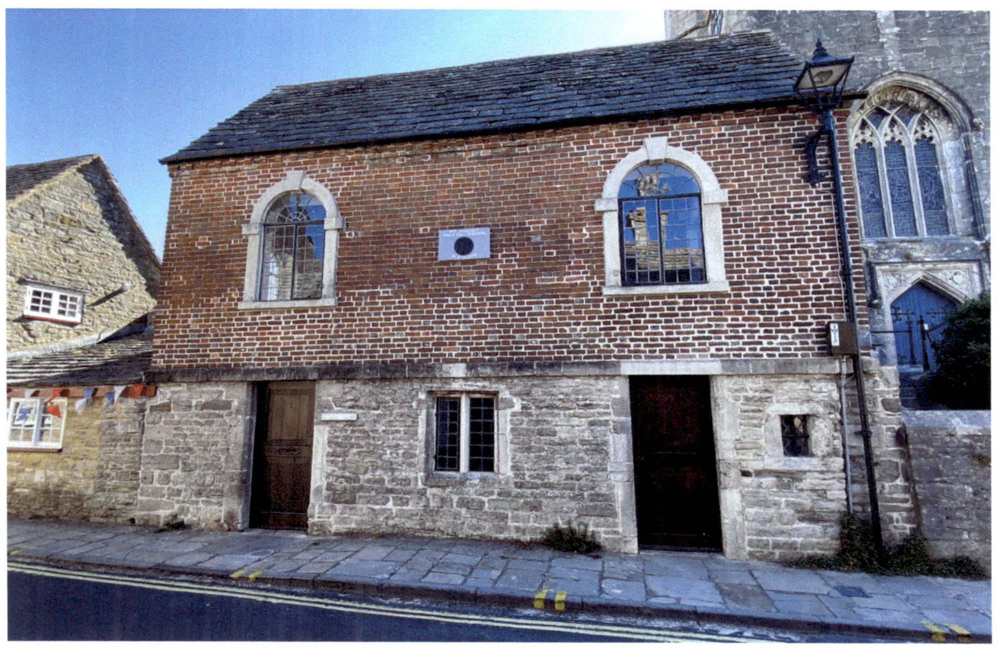

Corfe Castle Town Hall is reputed to be the smallest in England.

make the pilgrimage to Ower Farm by car instead. On arrival, being Shrove Tuesday they generally receive a pancake in return for their peppercorn.

Ower Quay has long since sunk into the mud of Poole Harbour, but in medieval times vast quantities of Purbeck marble and stone were exported through what was then the premier port on the Isle Purbeck. However, one remnant of these times does still remain and that is the overgrown track near Ower Farm, which is still called Peppercorn Lane and of course the term peppercorn rent is still in usage.

As with Purbeck marble, the Romans were also the first people to quarry the more functional but less ornate Purbeck stone in quantities of significance for building purposes. Quarrying continued after the Romans left and then started to become more important during the sixteenth century, when large manor houses were being constructed and the stone was valued for use as gables and mullioned windows. It was also in great demand for roofs, tiles, sinks and tombstones. Also many Purbeck villages such as Kingston, Worth Matravers, Langton Matravers and Corfe Castle, to mention only a few, look wonderfully picturesque as they have all been built with the stone, and new houses are still built with the local stone today.

Purbeck stone was in great demand in London after the Great Fire of London of 1666, when large scale reconstruction of the capital in stone was to be undertaken to replace the numerous wooden structures that had been burnt down. At this time, the most common form of quarrying around Swanage and the Purbecks, continuing right up until the 1930s, was underground quarrying. The area concerned tended to be within a 6- or 7-mile area extending from the coast, south of Swanage and west as far as Worth Matravers.

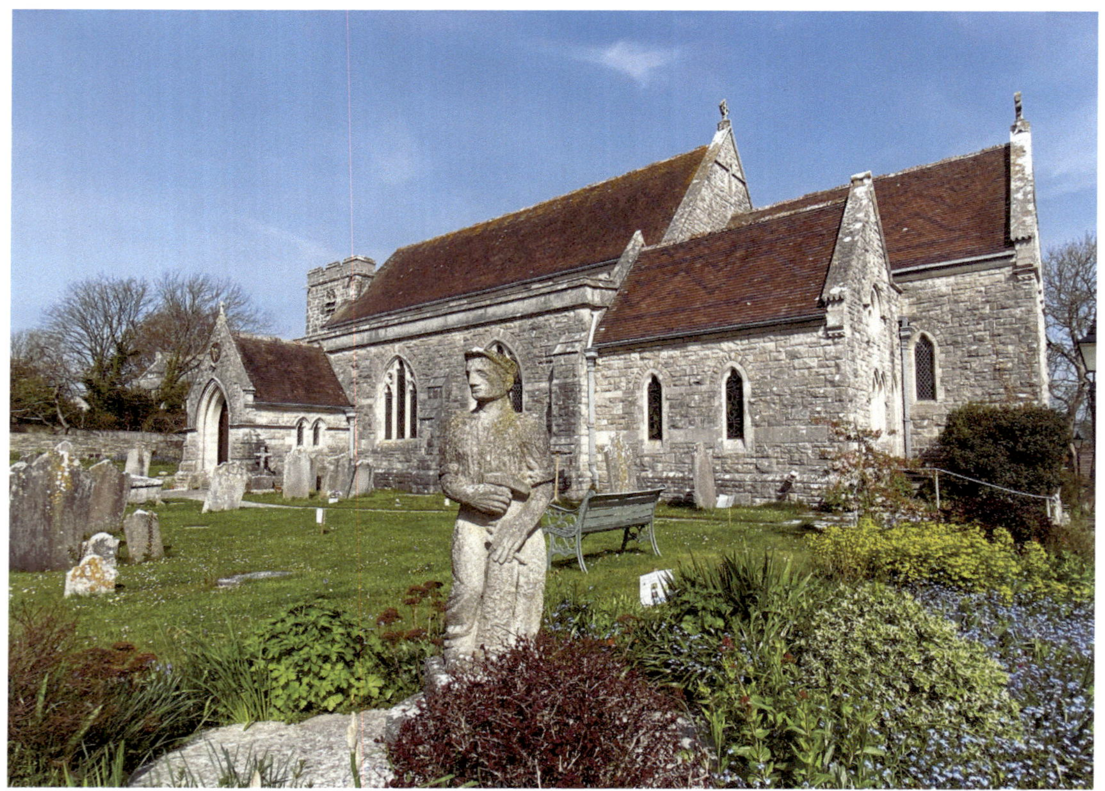

The statue in front of St George's Church, Langton Matravers, is titled 'Mason' and marks a thousand years of quarrying and stone working in the Purbecks. The statue was commissioned for the new millennium and was created by the sculptor Mary Spencer-Watson.

Initially the stone was quarried using a primitive form of open cast mining, in quarries known as 'quarrs' whereby quarrymen dug into the rock after having sought permission from local landowners. There were hundreds of these small-scale underground quarries, where quarrymen dug the stone manually.

However, in the halcyon days of Purbeck quarrying in the eighteenth and nineteenth centuries, the process became a little more sophisticated and inland quarrying involved sinking a shaft, from which a series of tunnels or lanes were dug leading from it. The quarrymen would then place the quarried stone into small carts also known as quarrs. Meanwhile, above ground, a horse or a donkey attatched by a yoke and chains to the end of a pole, known as a spack, which in turn was linked to a winch or capstan, would walk in a continuous circle and thus wind the chain around the capstan post, which in turn pulled the quarrs filled with stone up to the surface on a stone ramp. These more efficient quarrying techniques led to production to peak around this time and vast quantities continued to be shipped to London. Many of these old inland underground quarries are still visible now as rough areas of vegetation or trees, which block off the entrances to the old shafts in order to prevent cows falling down them.

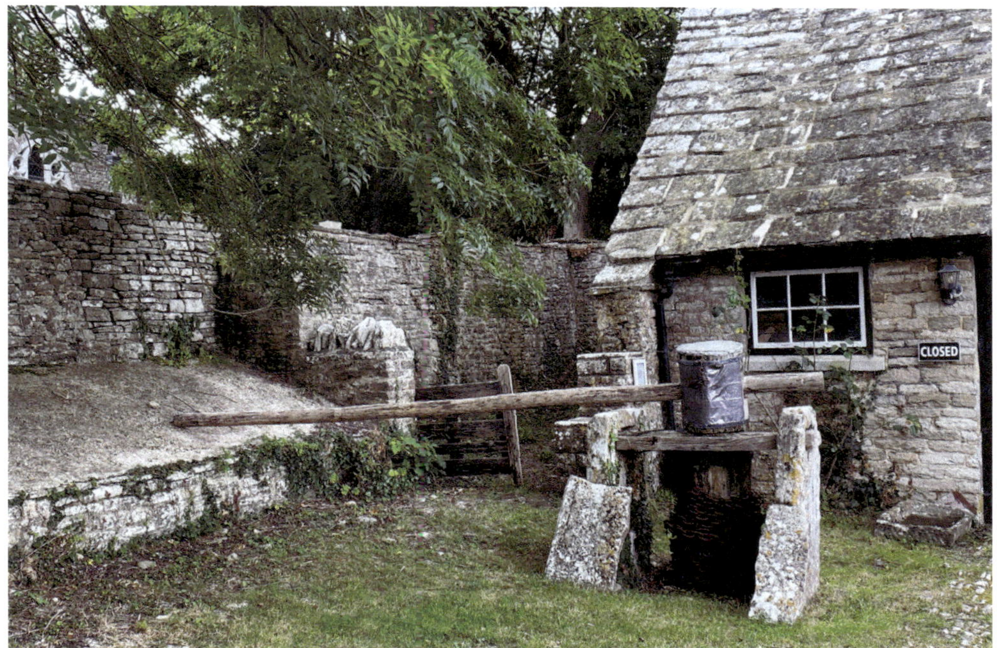

A replica of a capstan of the type that was used to haul up the stone from underground quarries in the eighteenth and nineteenth centuries is situated outside the Purbeck Stone Museum in Langton Matravers.

As demand grew in the seventeenth and eighteenth centuries, the more arduous and dangerous sea quarries were also developed. The spectacular remnants of the old abandoned mines can still be seen scattered along the coast between Durlston Head and St Aldhelm's Head, where the quarrymen mined the Purbeck stone from the cliffs using punches, wedges and hammers. They were also skilled stonemasons and often worked the stone on site into building blocks, sinks and troughs.

The Purbeck stone, once extracted, was loaded onto horn carts and pulled by men to a platform by the sea, where it was lowered by wooden cranes called whims (the same as a derrick) and loaded onto waiting boats below. In turn these boats were rowed out to larger vessels anchored off shore, known as ketches, before being shipped to Swanage.

On arrival at Swanage the stone was transported by horse and cart to the appropriate position on the quay in an area known as the 'bankers', which extended from the Stone Quay to what is now the Mowlem Theatre. Here the stone was sorted and laid out in piles ready for export all over the world.

When the stone was due to be moved from the bankers it was transported, again by horse and cart, this time wading into the water to waiting ketches, which in turn transferred the stone to larger ships waiting in deeper water.

Later in 1859, the tramway and pier were built in order to transport the stone on horse-drawn carts and make it easier to get the stone out to ships in the bay. The tramway survived until the 1930s and was latterly used to transport fish.

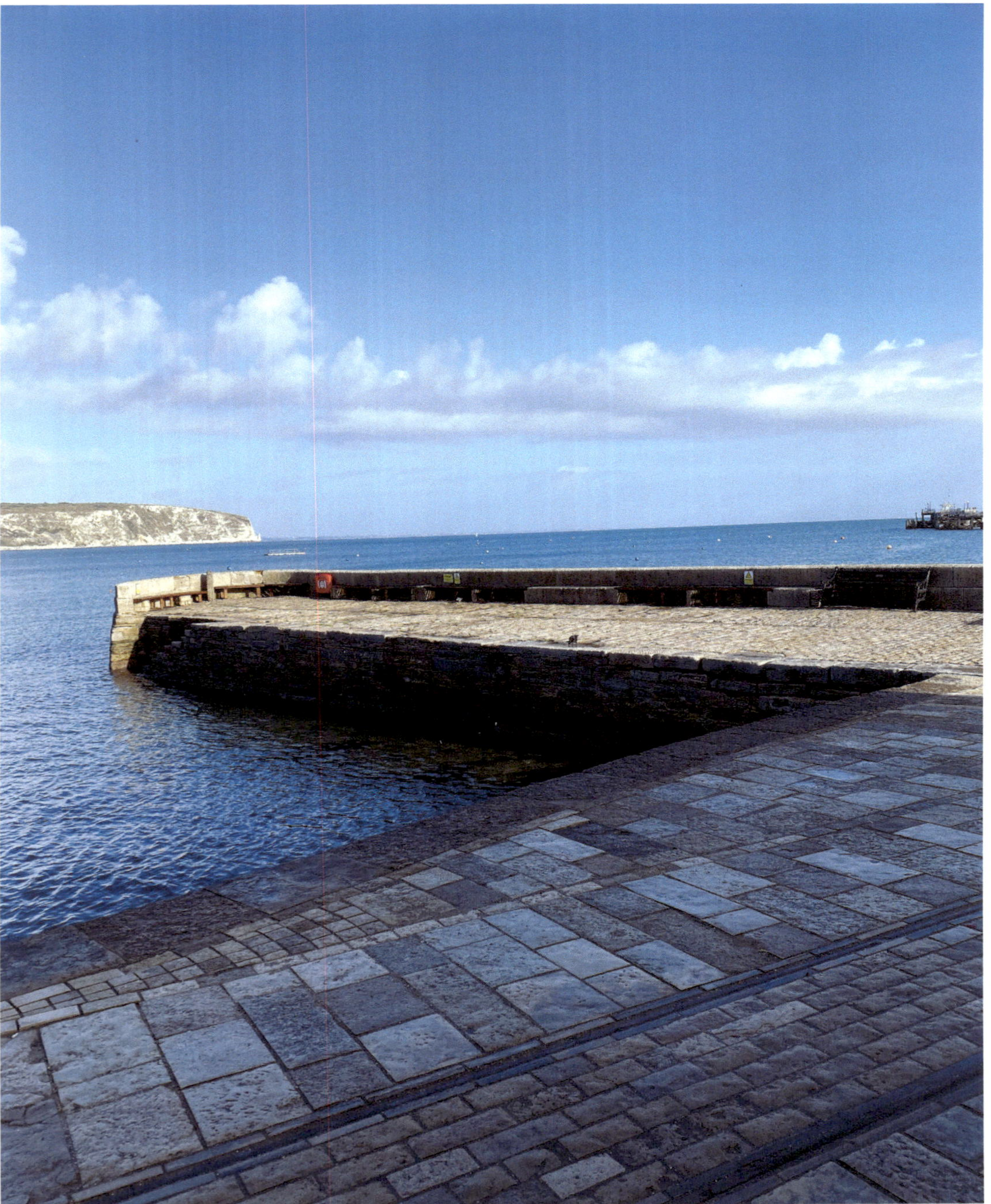

Stone Quay, Swanage, was built in the early nineteenth century at the instigation of William Morton Pitt MP for use by the stone and fishing industries. The quay and bankers enabled ships to load up directly from the Swanage seafront, whereas before this, the quarried stone had to be transported to Poole for shipping. The remains of the stone tramway that was originally used to transport the stone by horse-driven trams can still be seen.

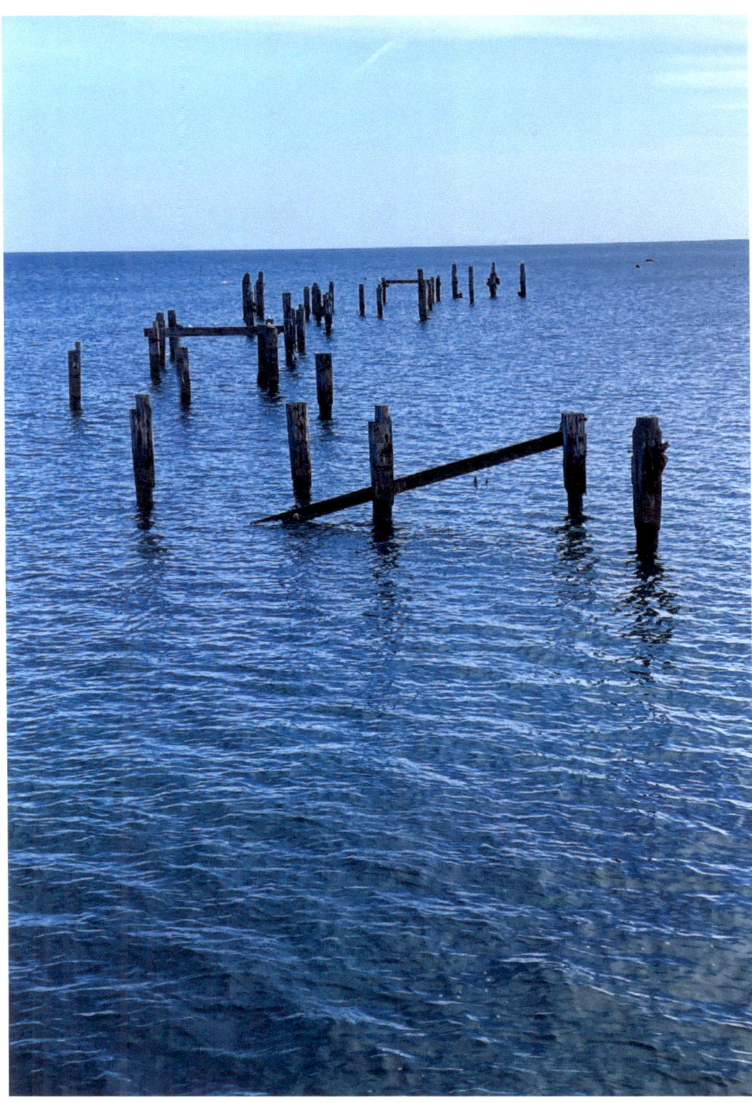

The remains of the
old wooden pier.

Tilly Whim Sea Quarry

The Tilly Whim Quarry, 1 mile south of Swanage near Anvil Point and within Durlston Country Park, consists of three stone quarries. They are the most easterly of the coastal quarries and are thought to have originally been open cast workings.

These quarries were mainly worked in the eighteenth century, before finally closing in 1812. The stone was hauled into ships waiting on the coast, using a whim, hence the name of these caves, named after a quarryman, George Tilly.

John Mowlem worked in these quarries alongside his family as a lad, then after the quarrying ceased, George Burt, who became Mowlem's business partner, opened them up as a tourist attraction. However, they were closed down in 1975 after a rock fall.

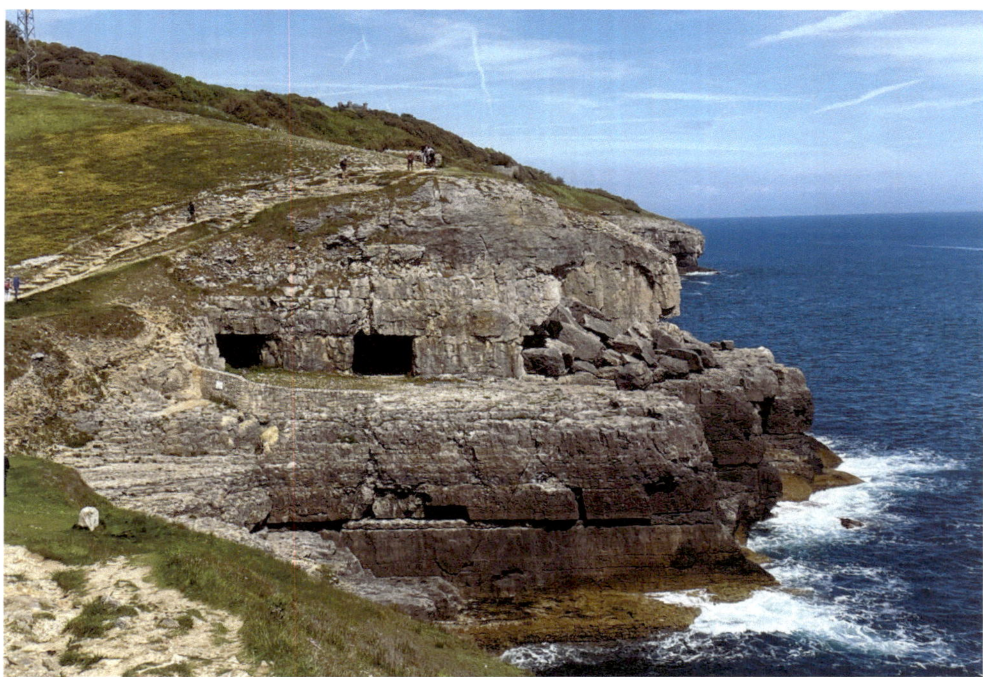

Tilly Whim Quarries.

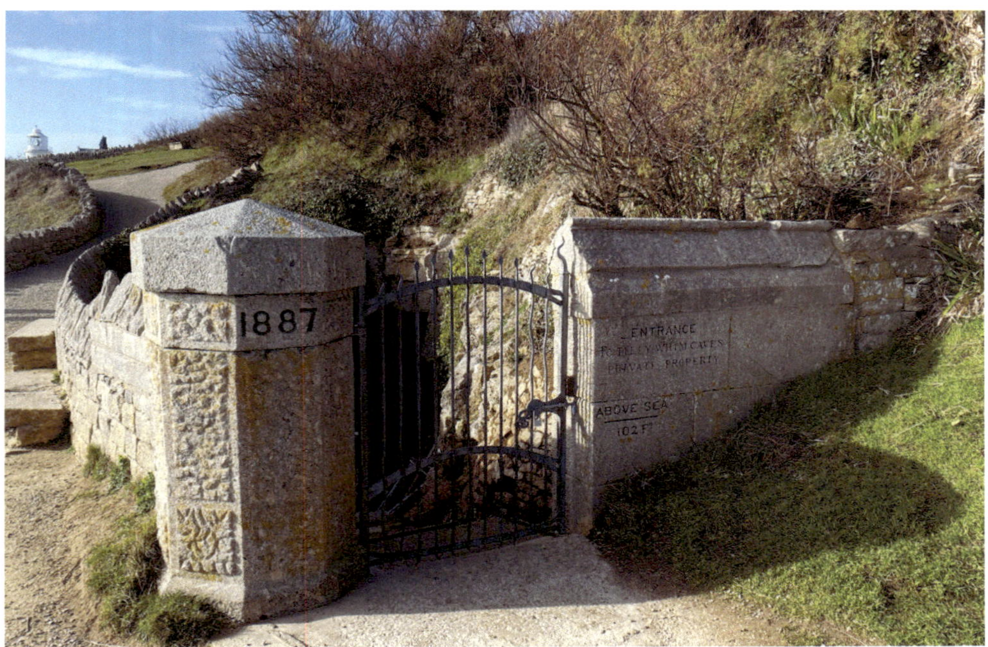

Tilly Whim, the granite boulder outside the entrance, was originally outside Pentonville Prison in London (see Chapter 2: Little London by the Sea).

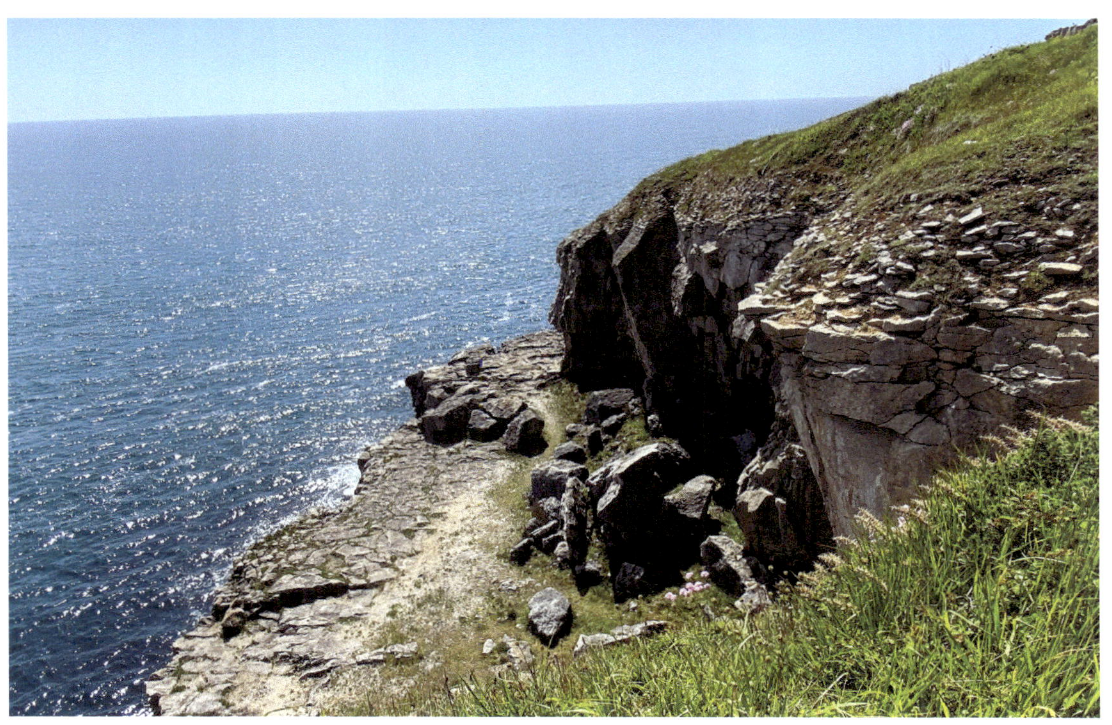

Tilly Whim ledge.

Dancing Ledge Sea Quarry

Some say that this spectacular former Purbeck stone cliff quarry is called Dancing Ledge due to the way the waves dance over the flat ledge at the bottom; others say it is because it resembles a dance floor. Whatever the truth, it is now a tourist spot, popular with climbers, fishermen, walkers and swimmers (in the man-made swimming pool) alike, where remnants of the industry are still visible in the form of the quarry caves, old tracks and ironworks.

Stone from here was utilised in the 1930s in the construction of Ramsgate Harbour in Kent and was transported there directly by ship.

The former quarry's other claim to fame is the man-made swimming pool, which was blasted out of the rocks in the early twentieth century for use by the school boys from Durnford School in Langton Matravers (now closed).

Hedbury Sea Quarry

To the west of Dancing Ledge, between Dancing Ledge and Seacombe, is Hedbury Quarry. It is a similar but more compact version of Dancing Ledge.

Seacombe Sea Quarry

Seacombe Quarry was another important source of Purbeck stone and was in operation from the eighteenth century until 1923.

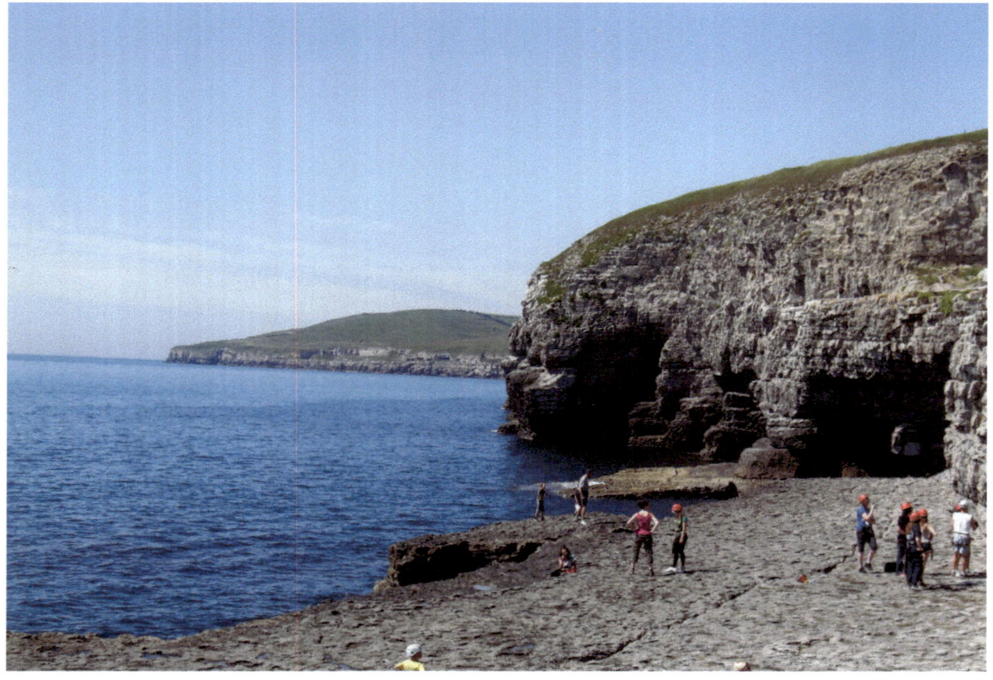

Dancing Ledge.

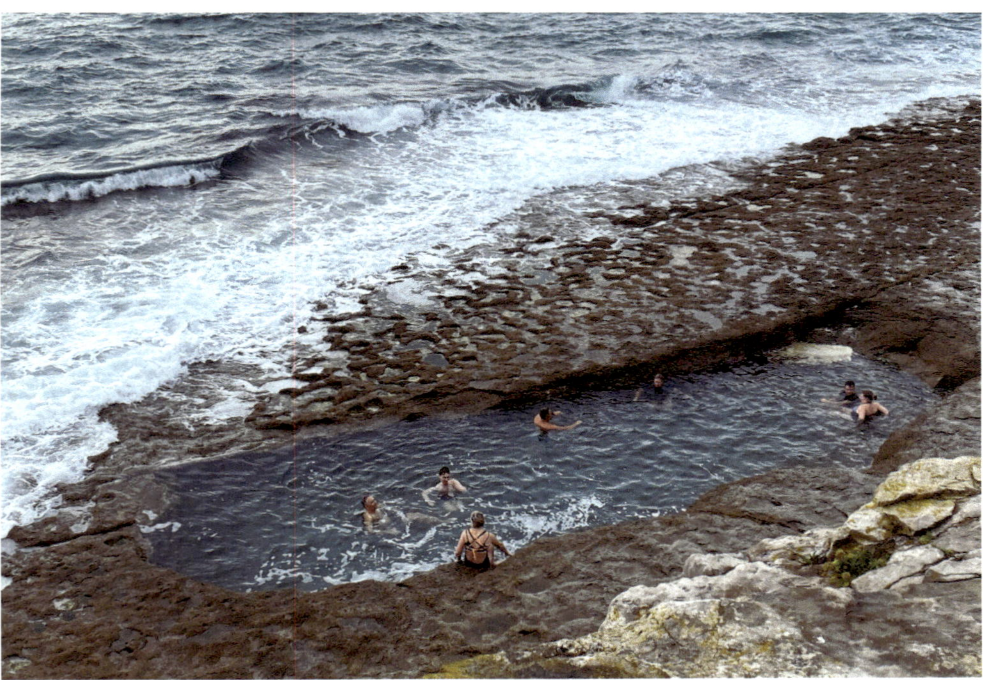

Dancing Ledge Swimming Pool.

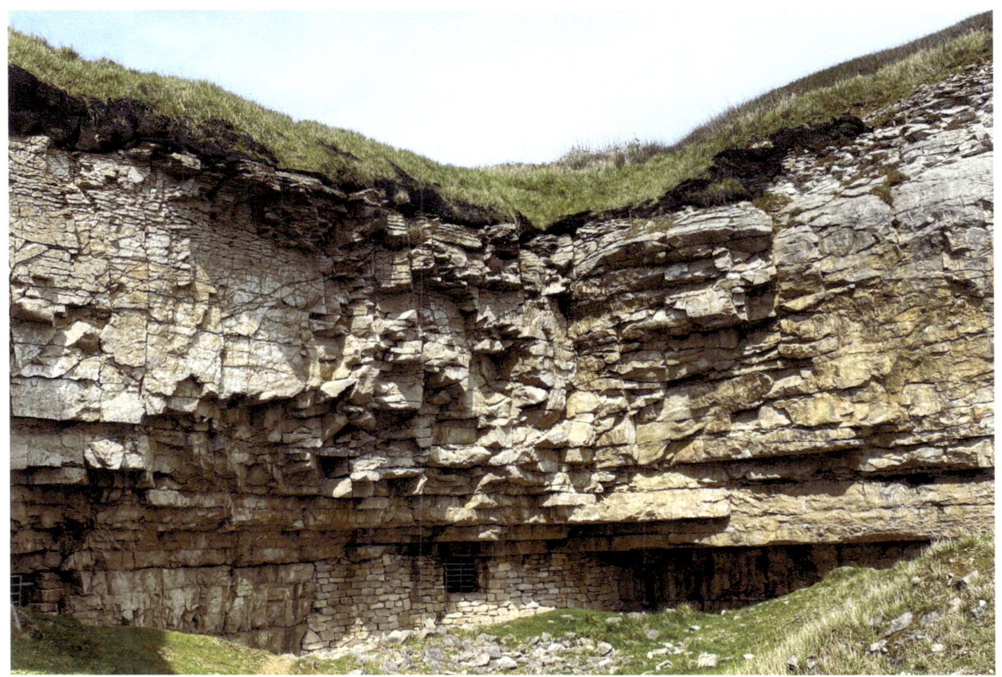

Dancing Ledge Quarry entrance.

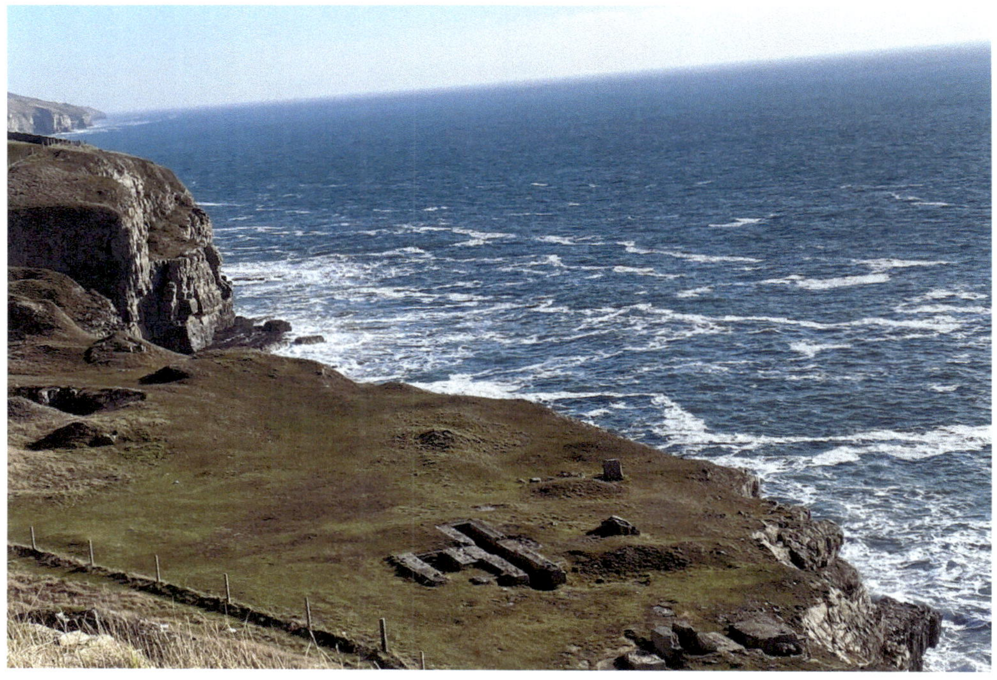

Hedbury Quarry.

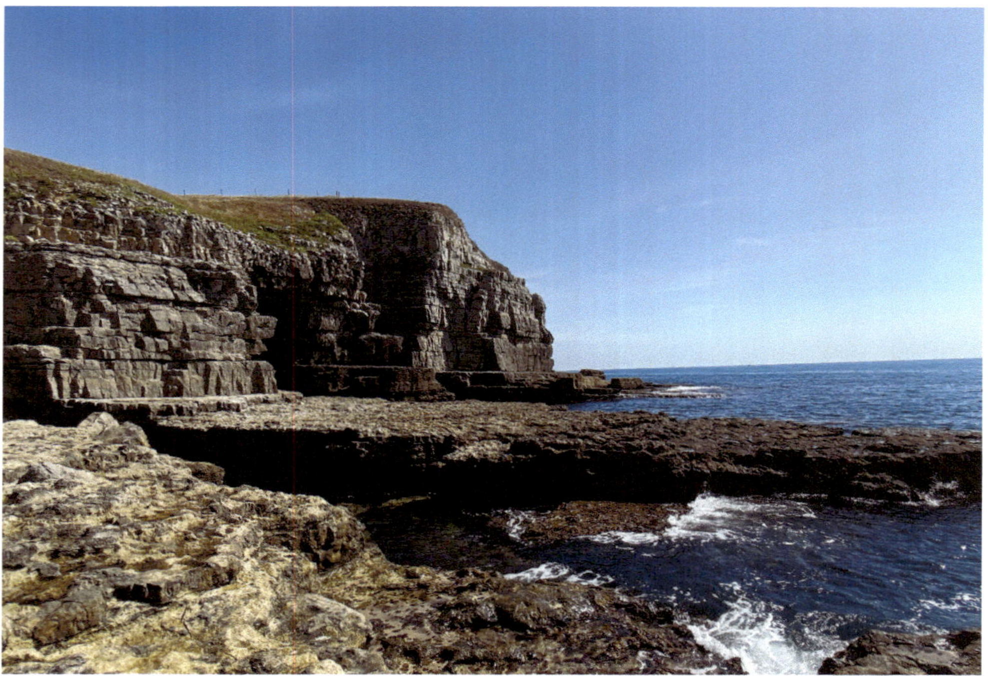

Seacombe Quarry.

Winspit Sea Quarry

The spectacular space age looking location, of these abandoned quarries near Worth Matravers, is such that it has had starring roles in programmes such as *Doctor Who* and *Blake's 7*. They were in use from 1719 until 1953.

Quarrying Today

Quarrying is still an important industry for the area today and vast quantities of Purbeck stone and marble continues to be extracted from the ground by open cast methods, before being transported onwards by lorry.

An example of a modern open cast quarry is Keates Quarry, which is adjacent to the Priest's Way between Swanage and Worth Matravers. A remarkable discovery was made in the vicinity by quarrymen Kevin Keates and Trevor Haysom in 1996, when they discovered dinosaur footprints, which are thought to have been made by brachiosaurus sauropods, a dinosaur which could grow to around 85 feet in length and weighed around 50 tons.

Purbeck Ball Clay

Another limestone deposit found in the Purbeck area around Swanage is Purbeck Ball Clay and again the Romans were the first to realise its potential. There were several Roman potteries in the Purbecks, resulting in the area becoming one of the largest and most important pottery manufacturing areas in Roman Britain. Wareham in particular

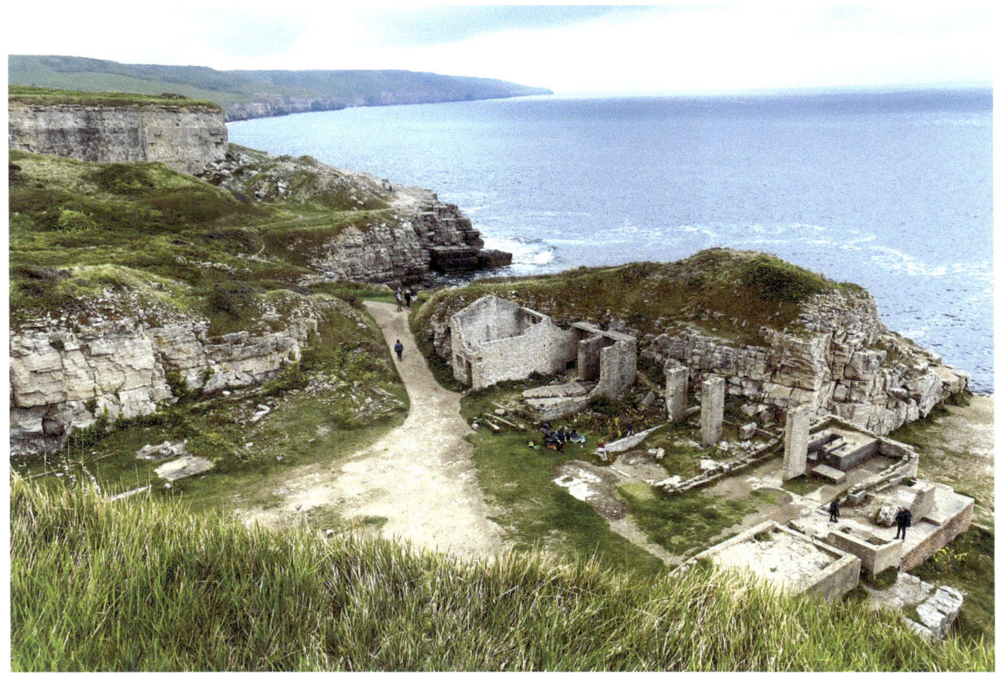

Old quarry buildings at Winspit.

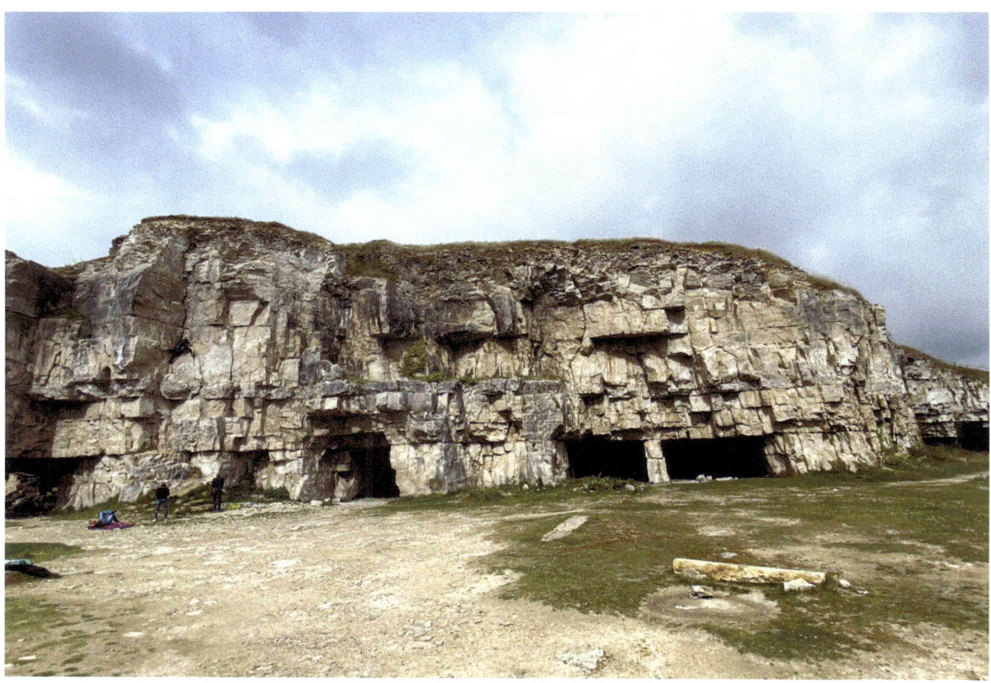

Winspit Quarry.

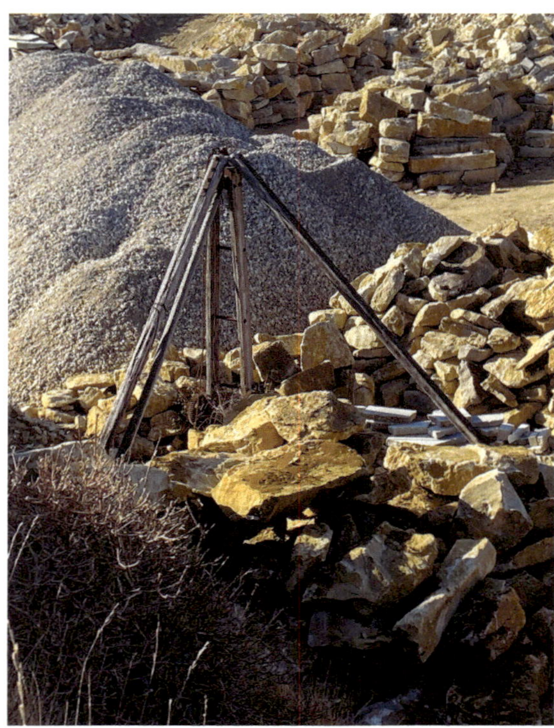

A hand-operated derrick or whim can be seen at St Aldhelm's Quarry, which is an open cast quarry slightly inland from the headland and still very much in use today. The derricks or whims were once extensively used in the cliff quarries of the Isle of Purbeck to lower stone onto the stone ships, but this is the last one remaining anywhere in Dorset.

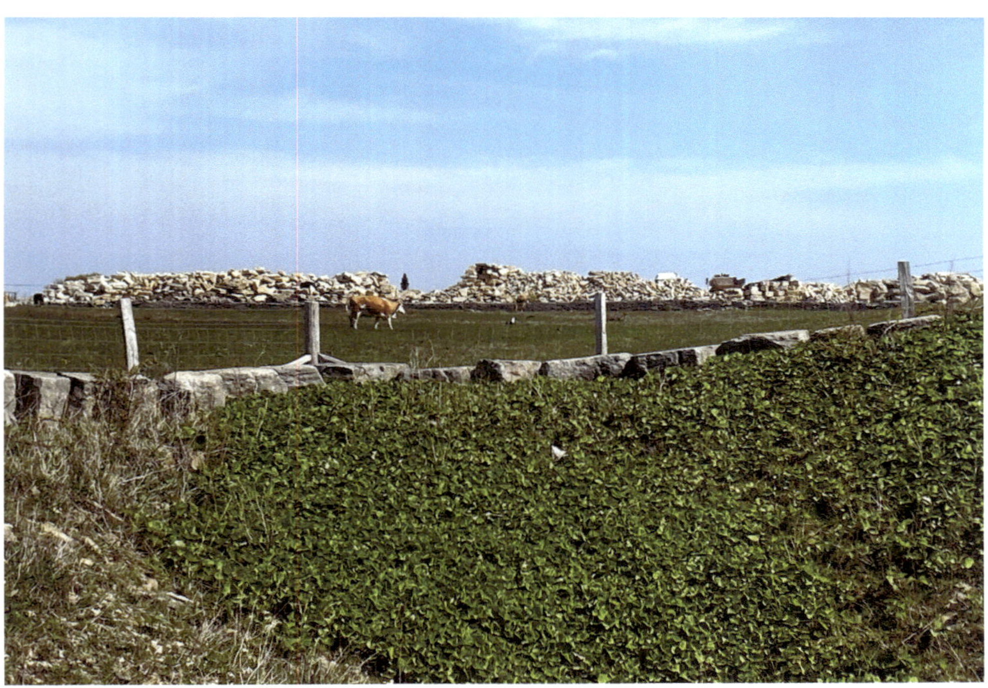

Keates Quarry.

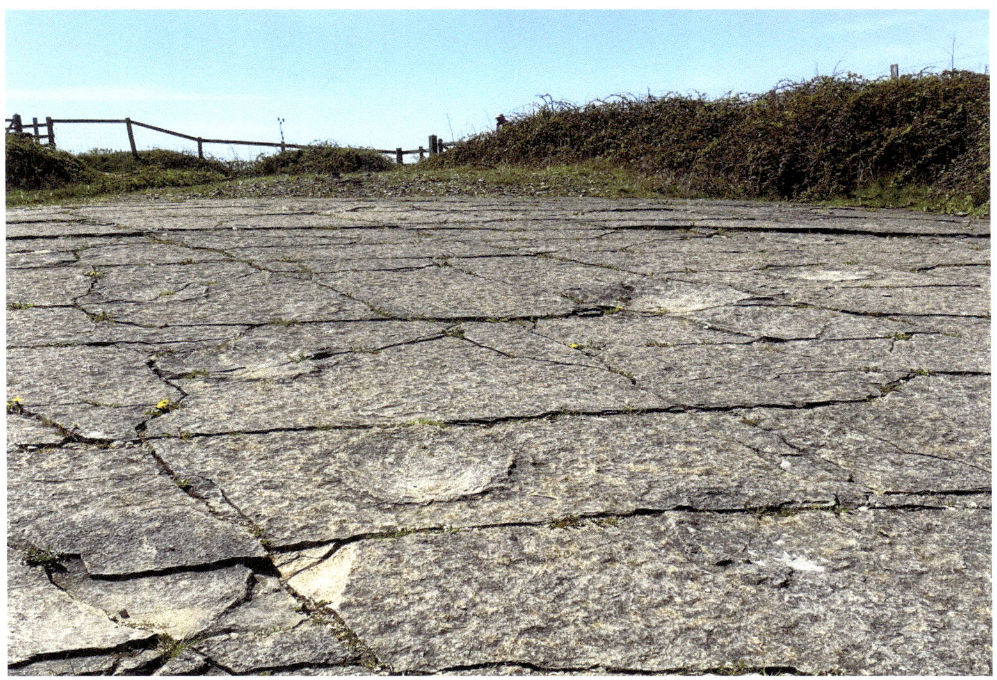

Dinosaur footprints.

boasted several potteries including large sites on the banks of the River Frome at Worgret and at Bestwall.

These potteries produced millions of black shiny pots and other items to satisfy the Roman's sophisticated style of living, such as bowls, plates, cups, dishes, jugs and cooking utensils. These were known as black burnished (polished) ware. The merchandise was exported all over Roman Britain and was also supplied to the Roman army. It has even been found as far north as Hadrian's Wall, 300 miles away.

After the Romans left Britain, the industry continued to develop and really took off during the eighteenth century. The industry benefitted from various modernisations such as the use of potters' wheels and kilns, resulting in greater commercial use for the product and consequent large-scale extraction, principally in the area between Corfe Castle and Wareham.

A further catalyst for the Purbeck clay industry in the eighteenth century was that it was regarded as the world's finest clay by Mr Joshua Wedgewood, as it possesses the vital quality of plasticity making it easier to work with and also doesn't shrink when fired. Accordingly, vast quantities were mined at Arne and carried by donkey or packhorse to sailing barges at wharves on the River Frome at Wareham, as well as to wharves on the south side of Poole Harbour. It was then shipped around the coast to the River Mersey and then transported by canal to the Staffordshire potteries.

Also at around this time the ball clay was in great demand for its suitability in the manufacture of tobacco clay pipes.

Today Purbeck ball clay is used in making everyday articles including wall and floor tiles, washbasins, toilet bowls, plates, cups, saucers, acoustic ceiling tiles, linoleum, insulated electrical cables, pale coloured bricks, clay drainage pipes, windscreen wipers, spark plugs, engine mountings, hoses, fertilizers and many others. It is processed at the Furzebrook plant of Imerys and approximately 80 per cent of it is exported.

Local Transport Hubs Associated with the Clay Industry Before Lorries Became the Preferred Mode of Transport

Furzebrook

Furzebrook was a processing centre, where the Purbeck Ball Clay was turned and ripened in order to increase its malleability. In its day, several narrow gauge light railways bringing clay from outlying pits converged here and then went onto the wharf at Ridge. Two major operators were involved in the industry at that time: the Pike brothers and Benjamin Fayle. Each had their own railways, but joined forces in 1949. The railway continued to operate until 1956, when road transport became a cheaper option.

The railhead at Furzebrook is now used to transport the oil extracted from the Wytch Farm oil well.

Ridge on the River Frome

Ridge, a wharf on the River Frome near Wareham, was a major transport hub for Purbeck Ball Clay. The clay was transported by light railways from the Purbeck Ball Clay pits, initially to Furzebrook to ripen and then to Ridge where it was transferred to barges, which were then towed by tugs to Poole Quay, before being placed in ocean-going vessels.

The old wharf has now become a marina.

Middlebere Quay and Light Railway

DID YOU KNOW?
Purbeck was at the heart of the Industrial Revolution and that Dorset has Josiah Wedgewood to thank for its first railway.

Josiah Wedgewood ordered vast quantities of Purbeck Ball Clay for use in his pottery factories in Staffordshire. Initially the clay was delivered by canal boats pulled by horse and cart. However, the transportation of clay was revolutionised in the nineteenth century, when the donkeys and packhorses were put out to grass, as light railways took over to provide swifter and more efficient transportation, leading to the construction of Middlebere Quay, on Middlebere Creek, south of Arne on Poole Harbour.

The railway, built by clay merchant Benjamin Fayle, was used to carry clay from pits at Norden near Corfe Castle to Middlebere Quay.

Both the railway line and the quay closed in 1907 and all that remains of the old quay now are the timber stumps of the old Jetties.

Quicklime

In the nineteenth century, limestone was also used in the production of 'quicklime', which was mixed with water to produce slaked lime, an important ingredient of mortar. It could also be used as 'lime wash', which was used in much the same manner as paint is today. The quicklime was also frequently used as fertiliser and was spread on to fields to reduce the acidity in the soil and promote plant growth.

The large limekilns were very much a feature of Dorset at that time and every manor would have had at least one. The quicklime was produced by the burning of broken pieces of limestone and coal which were laced in alternate layers within the kiln.

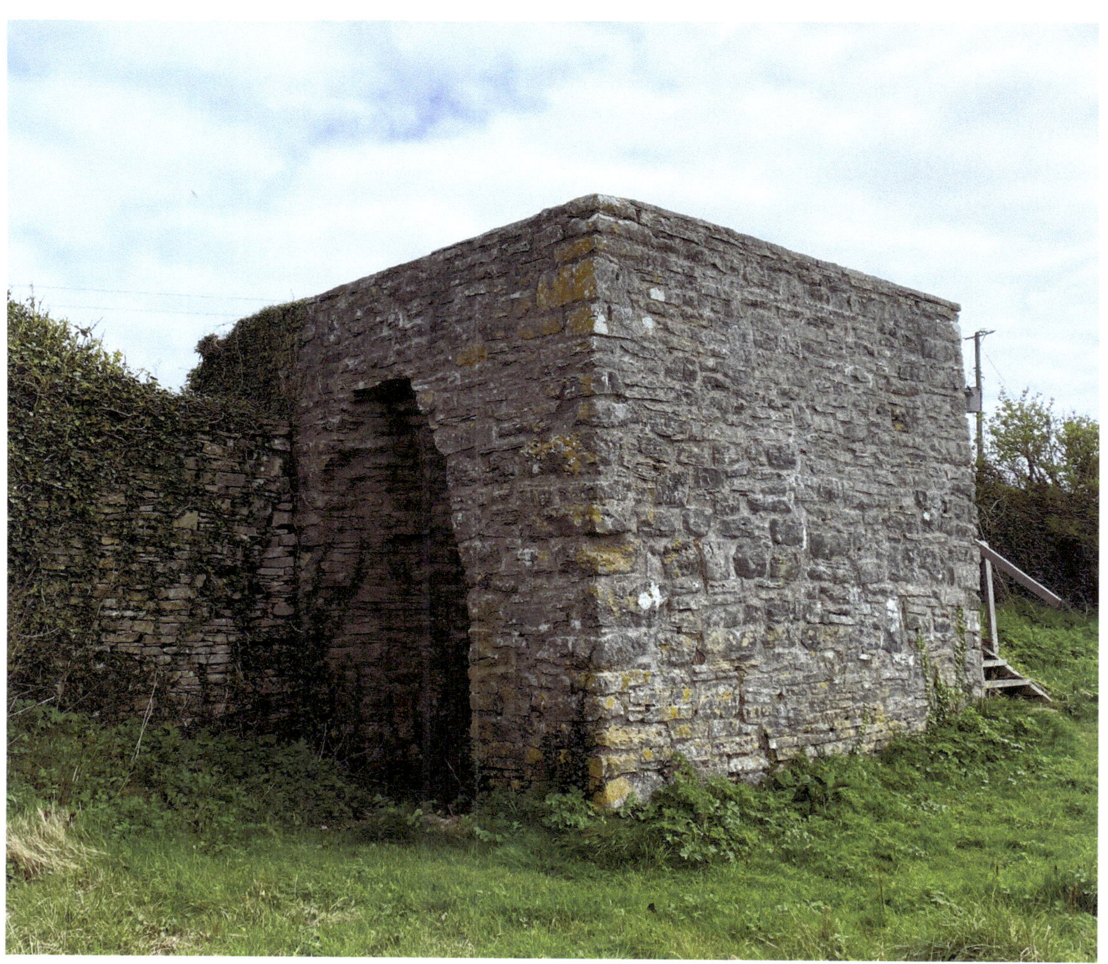

A limekiln on the Priest's Way, so called because it was the route a medieval priest walked between his two parishes of Swanage and Worth Matravers.

2. Little London by the Sea

Swanage contains so many buildings that once resided in London that it has gained the moniker of Little London by the Sea. The reason for this is that John Mowlem and his nephew, George Burt, had a proclivity for rescuing old London buildings and rejuvenating them in Swanage, where they then became part of the town's infrastructure.

During the nineteenth century, regular supplies of Purbeck stone and marble from local quarries were transported from Swanage to London, where much of it was destined for use by Mowlem and Burt in their London building projects. However, the returning large sailing vessels were considered unstable when unladen, so they were filled with ballast, which consisted of various items that Burt had sourced of unwanted masonry and stone that had previously been old London buildings that had been demolished as part of the redevelopment of Victorian London.

John Mowlem (1789–1868), George Burt (1816–1894) and Joseph Freeman (b. 1816)

Sometimes likened to Dick Whittington, John Mowlem was the poverty-stricken Swanage lad who worked in the depths of Tilly Whim Quarry. At the age of eighteen, he asked the captain of one of the ships taking Purbeck stone to London if he would take him to the capital for three pennies? The captain declined the offer of payment from the pitiable urchin and took him at no cost. Mowlem wanted to see if the streets were paved with gold. Obviously they weren't, so instead he paved them with Purbeck stone and found his fortune.

At the time of John Mowlem's birth, Swanage was a village whose inhabitants were predominantly engaged in fishing, or, alternatively, quarrying the local stone and marble. The stone was brought from local quarries to the stone quay at Swanage, where it was piled up awaiting export to London and all over the world. He started his working life working in Tilly Whim Quarry alongside his father and three brothers and was mainly involved in lowering the stone down the cliff face onto the waiting barges. He then moved to London at the age of eighteen in 1807. As a quarrymen, he was also a skilled stonemason, so he managed to find employment at a firm of stonemasons and builders and his abilities soon saw him promoted to general foreman.

In 1822, he established himself in business as a self-employed mason, first near Pimlico Basin and shortly afterwards at Paddington Wharf, now known as Little Venice. Later in the 1840s, he asked two partners to join him: George Burt, his young nephew on his wife's side, and a Yorkshireman by the name of Joseph Freeman, who was married to George Burt's sister. Together they formed Mowlem, Burt and Freeman.

Shortly after their establishment they secured a major contract to re-pave Blackfriars Bridge and as they managed this task successfully, they were offered further contracts to re-pave London Bridge and the Strand. Then in 1844, at the age of fifty-five, John Mowlem retired and returned to his native Swanage, leaving the business in the very capable hands of his nephew, George Burt.

The business continued to flourish and the financial crisis of 1866/67 also worked in the company's favour as it saw the demise of other building contractors, leaving Burt free rein to mop up the majority of the big London contracts, including the building of Queen Victoria Street in the City in 1869, the rebuilding of Billingsgate Market in 1874, the City of London School in 1880, Smithfield Market in 1882, the Imperial Institute in 1887, as well as major sewerage, railway and tramway works. Mowlem Burt and Freeman never looked back and became the internationally renowned Mowlem Construction Company in the process. The firm existed until as recently as 2006, when it was acquired by Carillion.

In order to achieve this great success, they actually worked mainly in granite and bought granite quarries in Guernsey and Scotland. However, they also imported stone into the capital from other areas of the country including the Purbecks and during the nineteenth century, regular supplies of Purbeck stone and marble from local quarries were transported to London.

Swanage Buildings and Artefacts Instigated by Mowlem and Burt

London Bollards

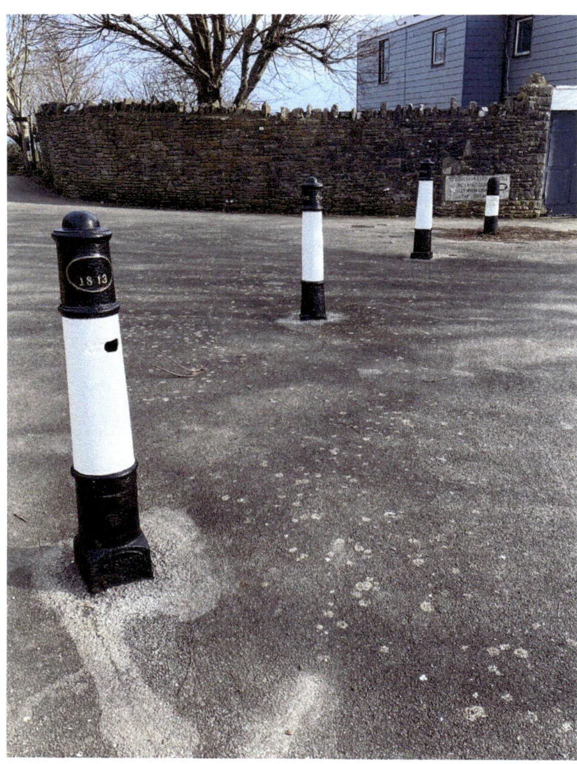

London bollards.

The most ubiquitous relics of 'Old London Town' that can be seen in Swanage are cast-iron London bollards, of which there are over a hundred dotted around the town. They originally date from the Battle of Trafalgar, as after Nelson's victory against the French in 1805, the British stripped anything of value from the captured French ships, including numerous cannons. However, the cannons were too large to fit into British ships, so they were utilised instead as bollards in Regency London, where they proved useful in preventing carriages from mounting the pavements. This innovation found great favour with the capital's populace as it was seen as a way of recognising Nelson's famous victory and also the subsequent defeat of Napoleon at the Battle of Waterloo in 1815. Indeed the bollards were so popular that when the original cannons were no longer available to replace bollards that had fallen into disrepair, replicas were made instead. In fact they have become an iconic feature of London and are still made today.

Although most of the Napoleonic bollards that were originally installed in London have been replaced over the years due to wear and tear, a few still remain, including one on the South Bank near to Shakespeare's Globe Theatre. Still luckily there are plenty that found their way to Swanage as ballast courtesy of George Burt, particularly in Durlston Country Park and outside the Town Hall. Some were removed for scrap metal as part of the war effort during the Second World War, but many of those that remain have the names of London parishes inscribed on them, such as St James', Clerkenwell, St Giles and Bloomsbury.

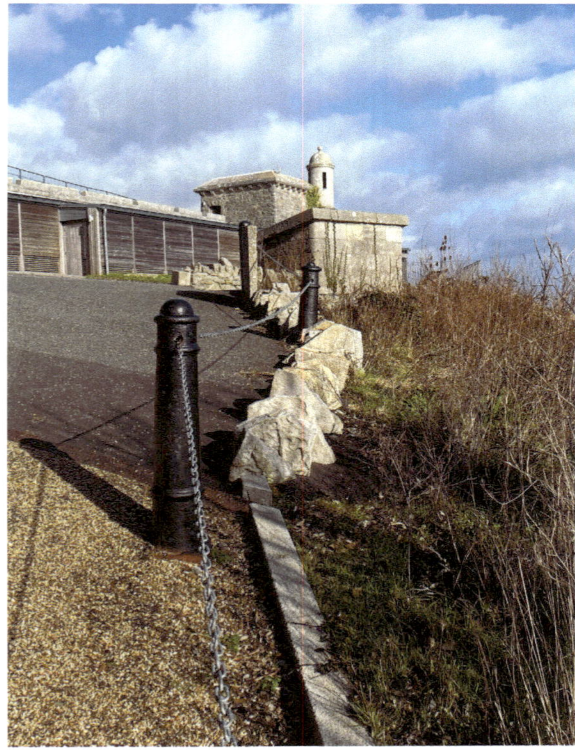

London bollards outside
Durlston Castle.

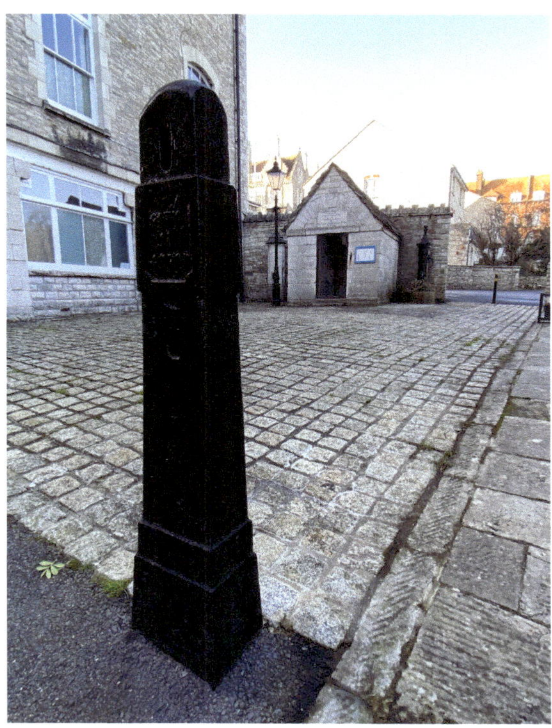
A London bollard in front of the old gaol.

Mowlem Institute

Upon his retirement, John Mowlem initiated the Mowlem Institute in 1863, which was a reading room to enable the working classes to educate themselves. It was constructed of local stone and was where the Mowlem Theatre now stands.

King Alfred's Memorial

During Anglo-Saxon times, England was made up of separate kingdoms, but they united under King Alfred of Wessex to defend against the ever-present threat of the Vikings from across the North Sea. Under his leadership, the Saxons were able to contain the marauders and then reclaim lands that had fallen under Viking control.

In AD 875, King Alfred the Great (r. 871–899) brokered a peace deal with the Vikings, which they later reneged on, meaning that by AD 877, King Alfred's Wessex men were again continually fighting off the Norsemen's constant raids, as they stood alone as the only kingdom in England still managing to hold out against the invaders.

This tiresome situation led King Alfred to develop a new strategy which involved thwarting the Vikings at sea before they could set foot on English soil, and in preparation for this he had overseen the construction of numerous ships, in what was the advent of the Royal Navy.

The strategy was put to the test when a fleet of Viking longships containing hordes of barbarians, which had been pillaging in Wareham a few days earlier, were spotted heading towards Swanage. To add to the defender's problems, a further fleet were also

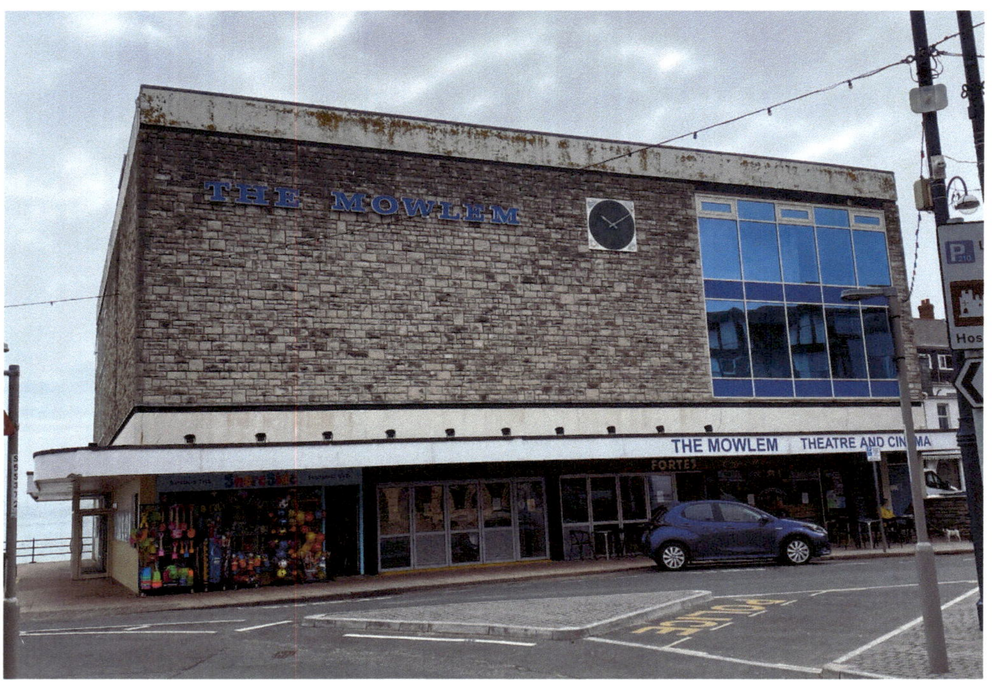

The Mowlem Theatre.

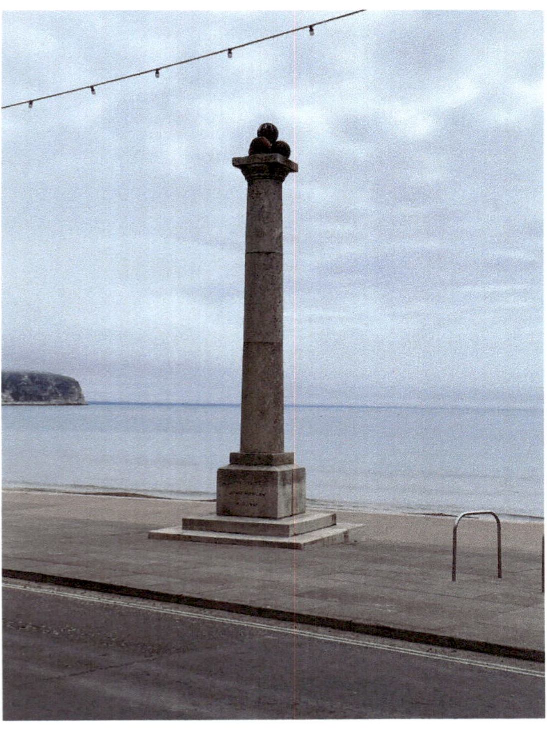

King Alfred's Memorial.

sighted making their way from Scandinavia. Alfred's ships and sailors put to sea in order to quell the threat and duly covered themselves in glory by sinking all 120 of them. However, some modern killjoy historians claim they were aided and abetted by a storm which drove the ships onto the Peveril Ledges.

In 1862, in recognition and celebration of King Alfred's great victory, John Mowlem instigated the construction of King Alfred's Memorial. However, the cannon balls on top of the monument are of no significance to this battle, but instead were fired at British ships by the Russians during the Crimean War.

Gaol

At the end of the nineteenth century, before the advent of police cells, small lock-up cells tended to be used to combat drunken, antisocial behavior, vice and immorality on the streets. In 1803, John Mowlem initiated the erection of the Swanage gaol just behind the Town Hall, which was paid for by public subscription and can still be seen today.

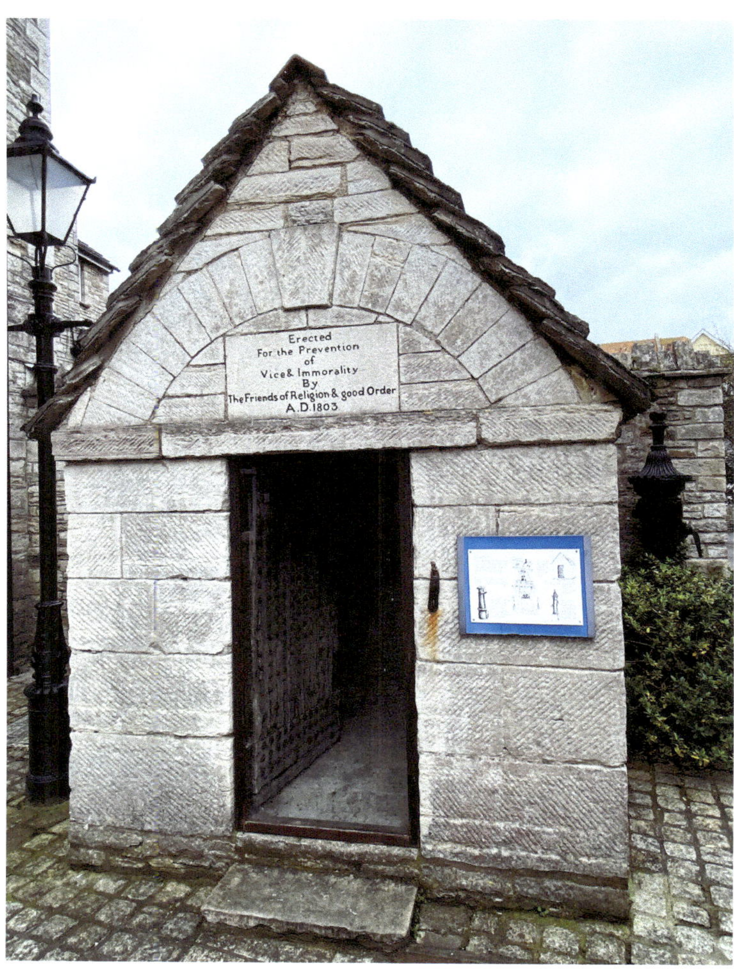

Town gaol.

Town Pump

The cast-iron water pump next to the gaol was installed by George Burt in 1881. The Church Hill Cross nearby, which commemorates Sir Reginald Palgrave (1829–1904), the clerk of the House of Commons, marks the site of the original town water pump.

Town Hall Façade

In 1881, renowned Dorset architect George Crickmay designed Swanage Town Hall on land purchased for the purpose by George Burt. However, the end result didn't look particularly grand and in 1883, Burt added a façade which came from the front of the Mercer's Hall in London's Cheapside and had originally been designed by Sir Christopher Wren in 1670.

Mercer's Hall had been constructed shortly after the Great Fire of London and the appropriate authorities thought it cheaper to copy the stonework and replace it, rather than attempt to clean the years of London grime that had accumulated on the building. The Mowlem company was contracted to dismantle it and also to widen Cheapside. Burt, in his customary fashion, seized the opportunity and had the building transported to Swanage, where the sea air soon cleaned the grime from the building.

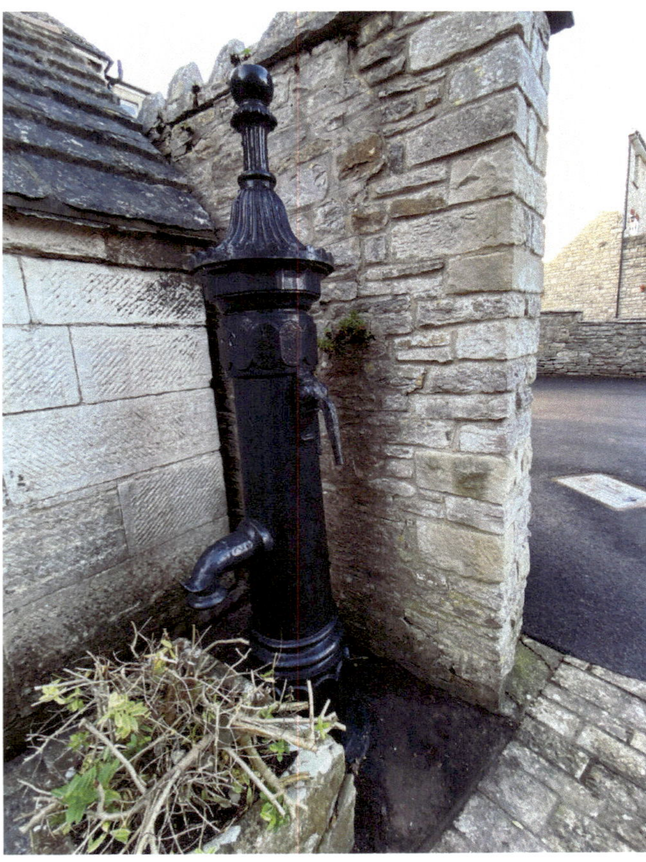

Town Pump.

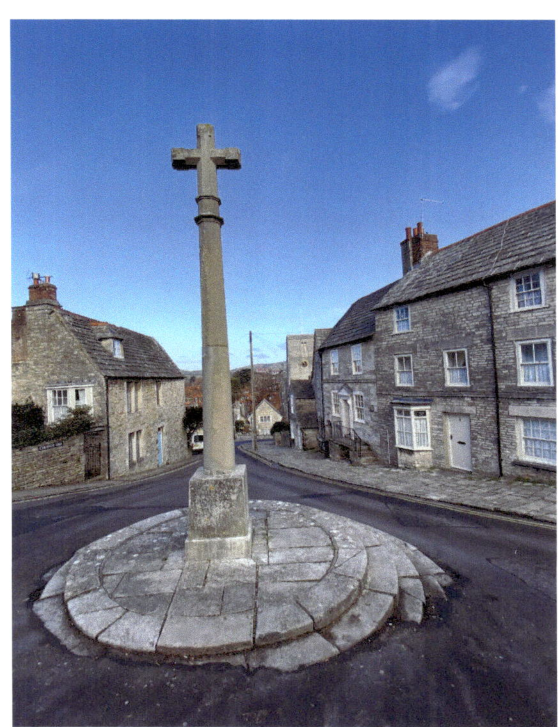

The Church Hill Cross is at the original site of the town's first water pump.

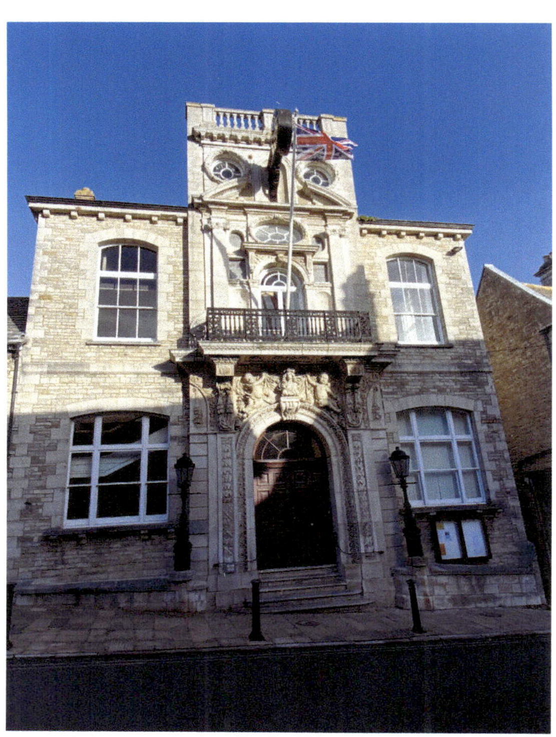

Town Hall.

When the new town hall was first built the basement housed the town fire engine and ambulance and was an open shelter supported by iron columns that had been removed from Billingsgate Fish Market in London.

Purbeck House Hotel

Almost opposite the Town Hall and equally as grand is a building that was previously a convent but was bought as a home by George Burt in 1857. He knocked the original building down and designed it in collaboration with the architect George Crickmay and between them they produced the majestic building we see today. The building is now a family-run hotel with eighty bedrooms.

Victorian Obelisk

The Victorian Obelisk on Ballard Down was originally erected by George Burt on its present site in 1883 to commemorate the introduction of fresh water to Swanage. However, prior to that, the structure was situated in Central London, outside the church of St Mary of the Nativity (also known as St Mary Woolnoth Church), on the corner of King William Street and Lombard Street near Bank station.

It was then temporarily removed from its site in Swanage during the Second World War as it was thought it could provide a landmark for the Luftwaffe, but was re-erected in 1973.

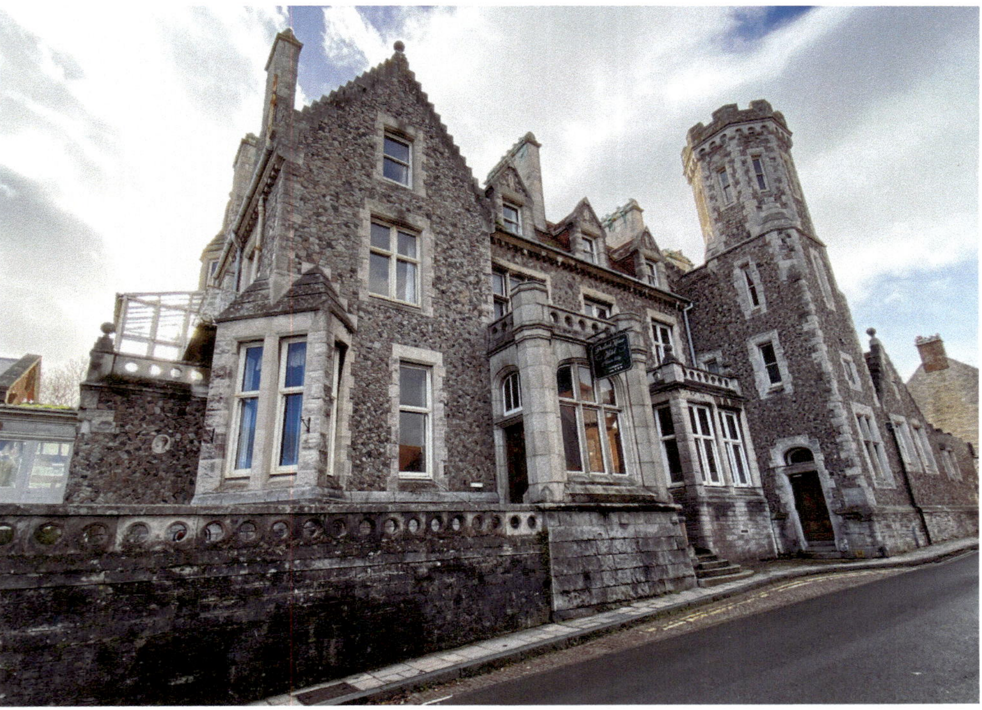

Purbeck House Hotel.

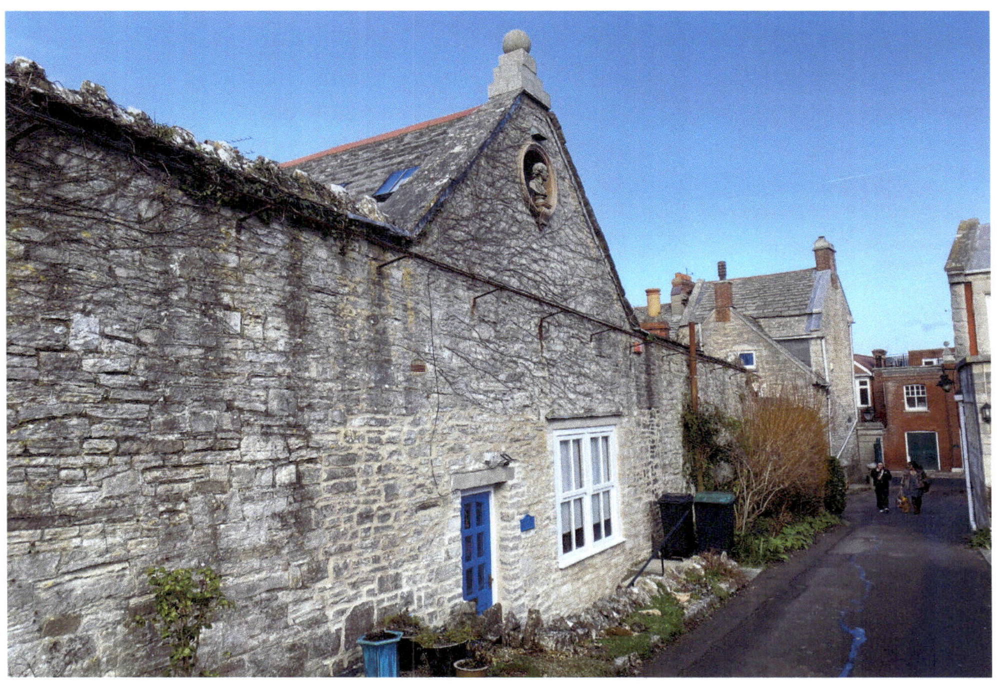

The remnants of the Old Convent are now Convent Mews.

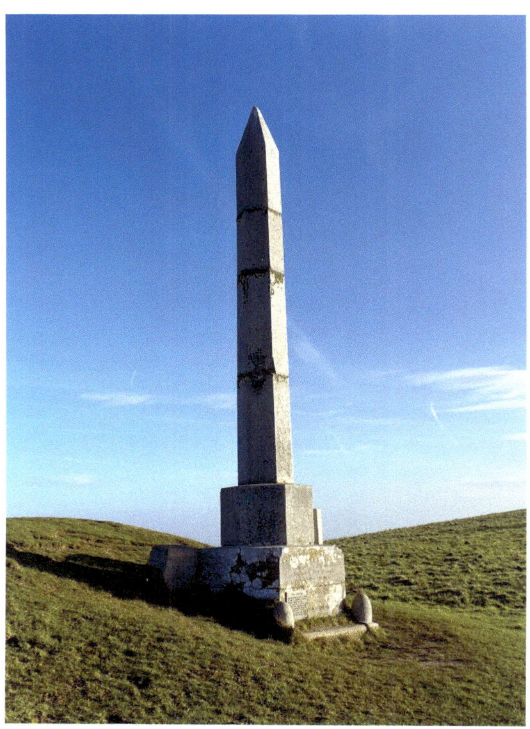

Victorian Obelisk.

Wellington Clock Tower

In the Peveril Point vicinity there is an extraordinary monument that in its previous incarnation had been erected in 1854 as a memorial to the Duke of Wellington and his victory at Waterloo. It was situated on the approach to the Southwark side of London Bridge. However, the Metropolitan Police were not overly enamored with the creation, as it provided in the police chief's words, 'An unwarrantable obstruction and didn't even keep very good time'.

It was no surprise then that Mowlem's offer to dismantle the obstruction was gratefully received and the individually numbered stones were duly transported to Swanage for re-erection, minus the clock and the spire, which did not make the trip.

The Old Pier

John Mowlem constructed the old pier in 1859, primarily as a means of getting Purbeck stone from the bankers out to the waiting ships more easily, but also to aid the shipment of timber, coal and fish. However, in 1885, the railway came to Swanage and offered an alternative.

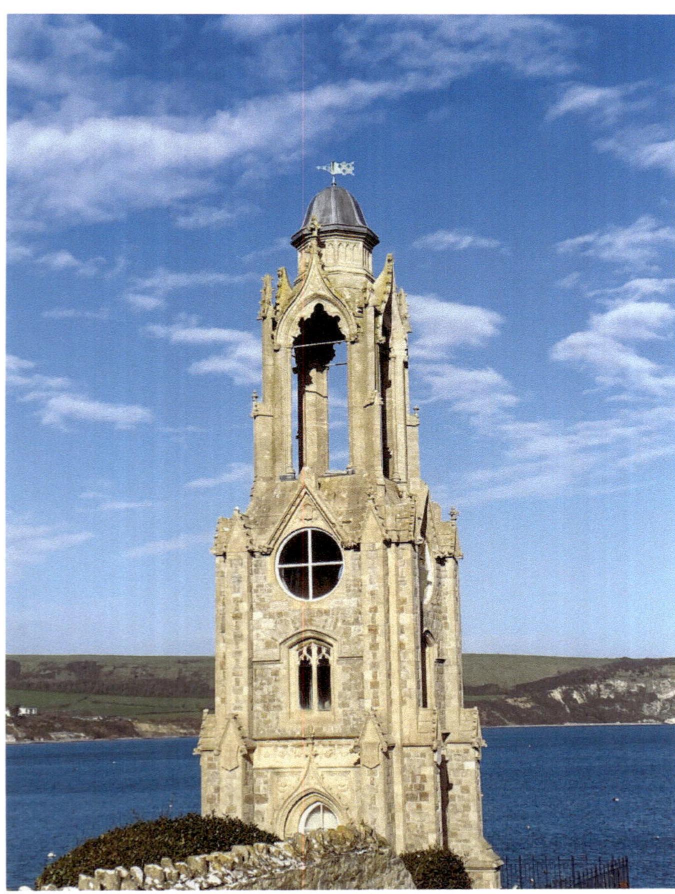

Wellington Clock Tower.

The New Pier

With the advent of the railways, Swanage became a popular resort for wealthy Victorians, resulting in the ever-resourceful George Burt accommodating the new fashion of paddle steamers, by instigating a service between Swanage, Poole and Bournemouth in 1871. However, it soon became clear that day trippers boarding pleasure steamers were not greatly appreciative of the close proximity of industrial stone boats and steamers loading up with fish and coal. Consequently a new pier was built in 1897, causing the old pier to eventually fall into disuse. Only a few wooden stumps next to the new pier are visible today.

The new pier is still in use today, but was temporarily removed during the war years as a precaution against the threat of invasion. It is one of only fourteen wooden piers remaining in the country.

The Prince Albert Memorial

The death of Prince Albert, Queen Victoria's consort, at the age of forty-two in 1861 was greatly mourned by the British public, who had appreciated his compassion and philanthropy.

George Burt advocated that Swanage should have a fitting memorial for the great man and in 1862, one year after Albert's death, Swanage was the first place to erect a memorial in his honour.

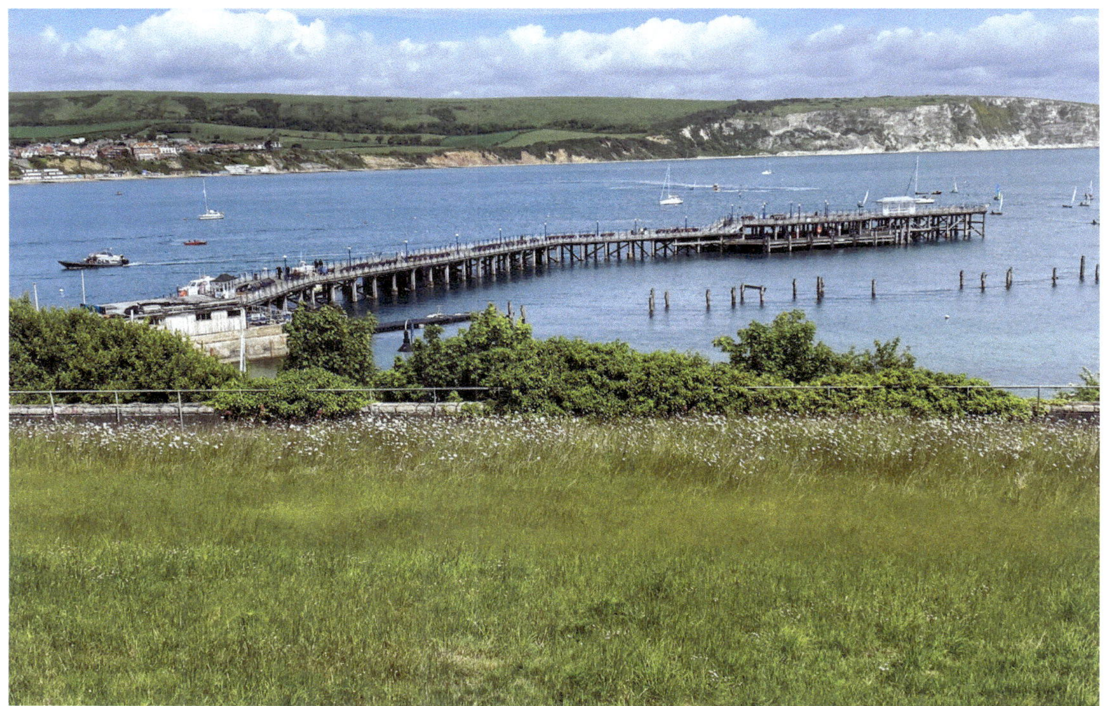

The new Swanage Pier with the wooden stumps of the old pier in the foreground.

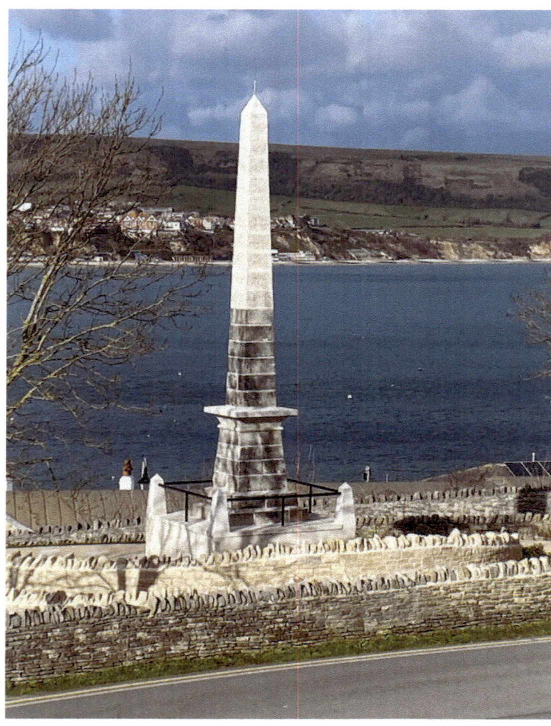

The Prince Albert Memorial.

The memorial, which was situated in the High Street, near to the current site of the British Legion, was built of Purbeck stone and was paid for by public subscription, despite the town only having a population of around 2,000 at the time. It is said that Burt modelled the design on an obelisk honouring the prominent City of London MP Robert Waitham that used to sit in Ludgate Circus in London, before it was moved to its current location in Salisbury Square, just off Fleet Street.

Queen Victoria visited Swanage in 1883 and when she made a point of stopping off at the memorial to pay her respects to her late husband, she was greeted by a sympathetic crowd of local well-wishers.

In 1971, developers removed the obelisk on the understanding they would re-erect it in an alternative location, which unfortunately, for whatever reason, never happened. It wasn't until fifty years later in 2021 that Swanage Town Council and the Swanage and Purbeck Development Trust charity secured planning permission to re-erect the monument close to Peveril Point, which is an appropriate site as Prince Albert once moored in Durlston Bay on the royal yacht and came ashore to take in the delights of Swanage around the Peveril Point area.

Swanage Railway

John Mowlem and George Burt managed to get a bill passed in Parliament that connected Swanage to the railway at Wareham, thus making the town far more accessible than previously. This along with the introduction of the new pier was to prove instrumental in

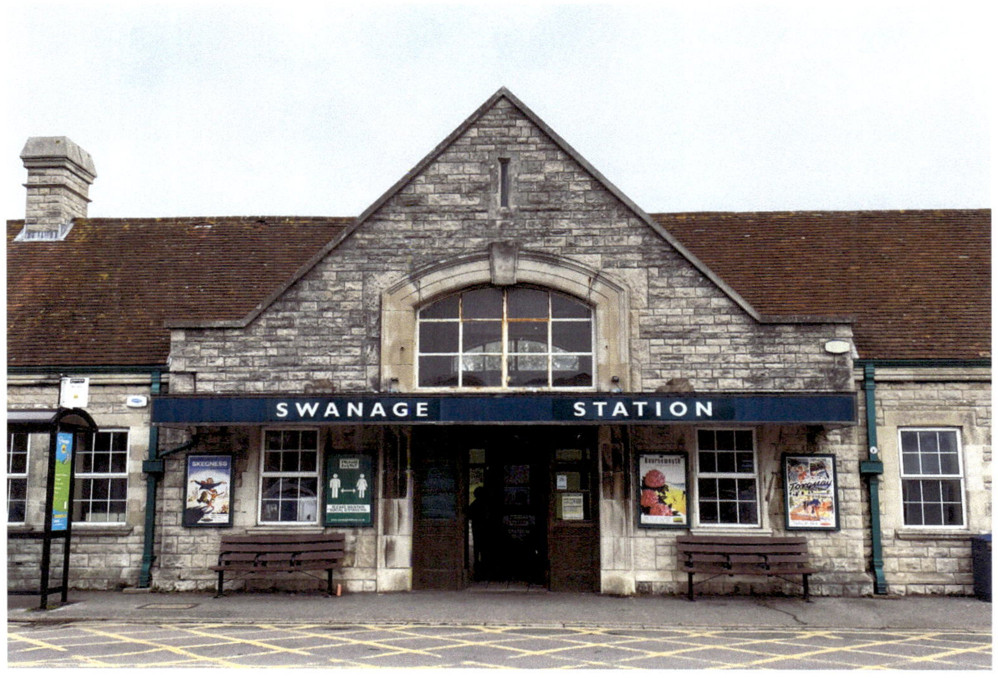

Swanage Railway.

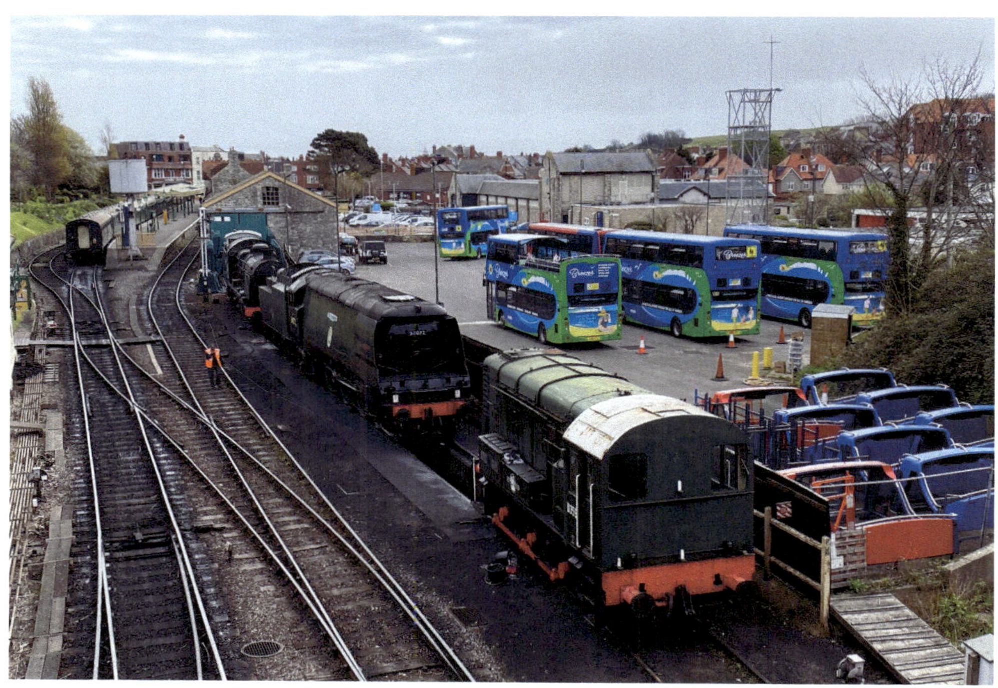

Swanage Railway.

Swanage prospering as a popular seaside resort. Sadly though, John Mowlem didn't live to see his railway project come to fruition in 1885.

The railway became a victim of the Beaching cuts in the 1960's, but has since been revived by volunteer steam railway enthusiasts, who have managed to create a regular heritage steam railway service from Swanage to Corfe Castle. However, although they have succeeded in getting trains running to Wareham on a sporadic basis, the dream of linking a regular service to the mainline services at Wareham again hasn't happened as yet.

Durlston Country Park

In 1863, George Burt purchased some rough semi-industrial land, featuring Tilly Whim Caves and numerous old stone workings on the cliffs near Swanage and transformed the area into Durlston Country Park.

Durlston Castle

Within the park, Burt incorporated Durlston Castle, which was built between 1887 and 1891 as the centrepiece. He also added numerous seats and stone inscriptions, as well as various old London artifacts such as London bollards and a cable that borders the castle garden, which was once part of a Thames suspension bridge. The castle was intended right from the start to be used as a restaurant and today it is still used as a cafeteria.

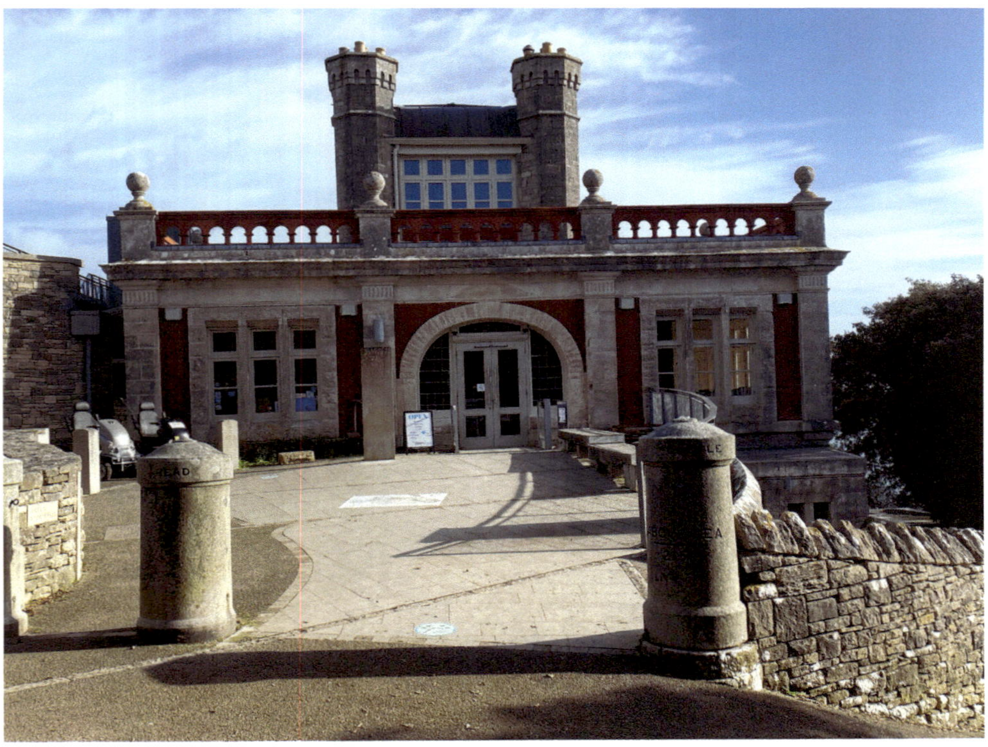

Durlston Castle – the granite bollards outside adorned Trafalgar Square in a previous life.

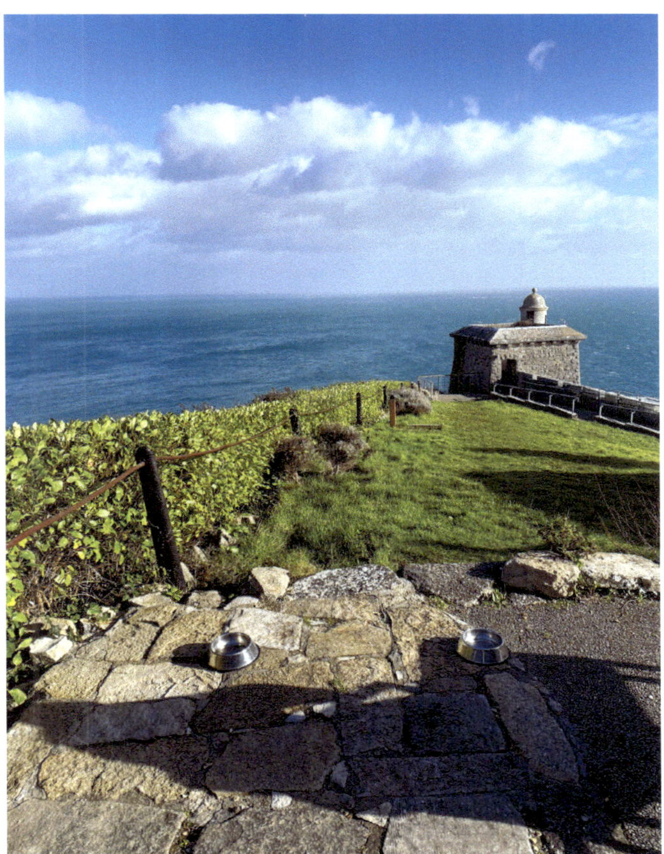

The cable at the edge of Durlston Castle Garden is attached to London bollards and was formerly a suspension cable on one of the Thames bridges.

The Great Globe

George Burt commissioned the great globe which is situated near Durlston Head within the grounds of Durlston Country Park, overlooking the cliffs in front of Durlston Castle. It weighs in at 40 tons and has a diameter of 10 feet. It is one of the largest and heaviest spheres in the world. It was constructed in 1887 at Mowlem's stone yard in Greenwich, London, and was brought to Swanage by sea. It is engraved with a 1880s map of the world, and also includes quotations from the Bible and Shakespeare.

Egyptian Seat

A stone bench known as the Egyptian Seat within Durlston Country Park was commissioned by George Burt in 1887. He drew his inspiration from a trip to the Great Pyramids in Egypt, where he had the audacity to upset the locals by attacking one of the great wonders of the world with a hammer and chisel, in order to try and understand how it was constructed. In his journal he writes, 'The astonishment depicted on their faces was very soon changed into an expression of excessive annoyance and I do not think that they were at all pleased by me bringing the piece away with me'.

The bench had begun to fall into a state of disrepair and has recently been refurbished.

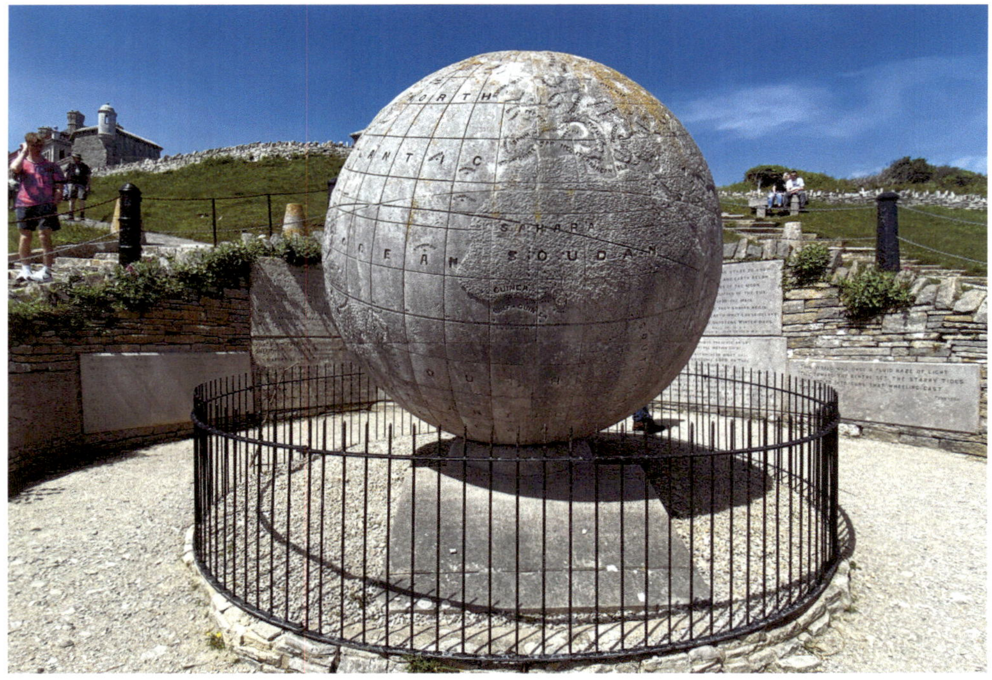

The Great Globe.

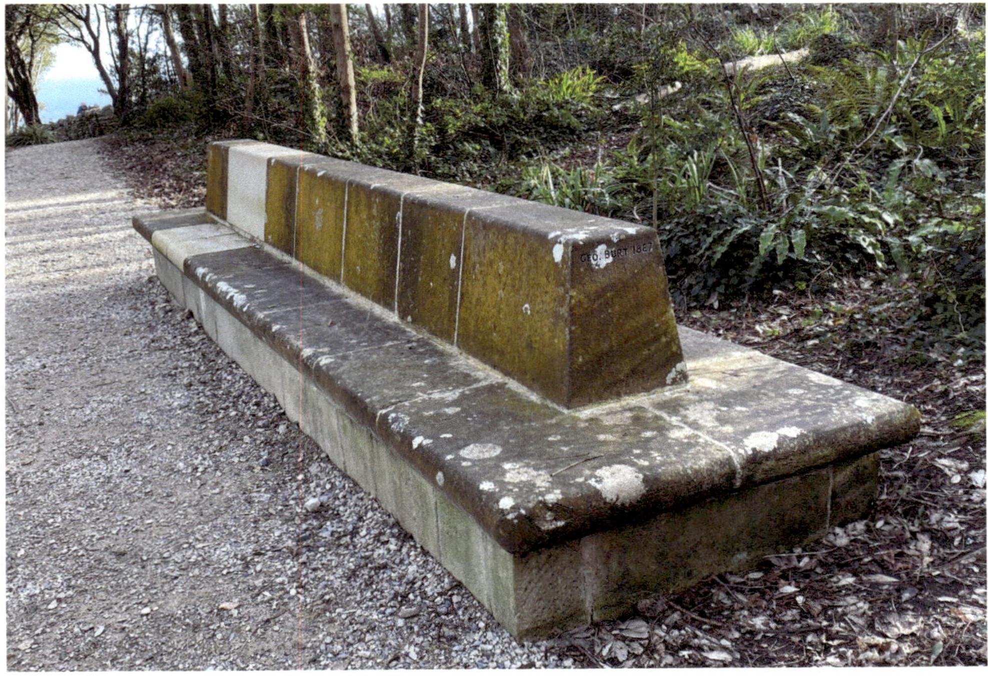

The Egyptian Seat.

3. Corfe Castle

The imposing stone fortress of Corfe Castle occupied a superb defensive position dominating the surrounding area and commanding the main route through the Purbeck Hills. It is a Grade I listed building and a Scheduled Ancient Monument. In its day, it was an impregnable fortress and one of the premier castles in England. It has a long and colourful history, which only ended when it was destroyed by Parliamentary forces in 1646 during the English Civil War.

The castle sits on a natural mound high above sea level and there is evidence that the site was occupied from early times, as the local landscape features Bronze Age barrows, Iron Age field systems, numerous Roman sites and also Saxon pottery.

The site first came to prominence as a royal Anglo-Saxon residence when King Alfred the Great (r. 871–899) turned it into a stronghold in order to protect the area from

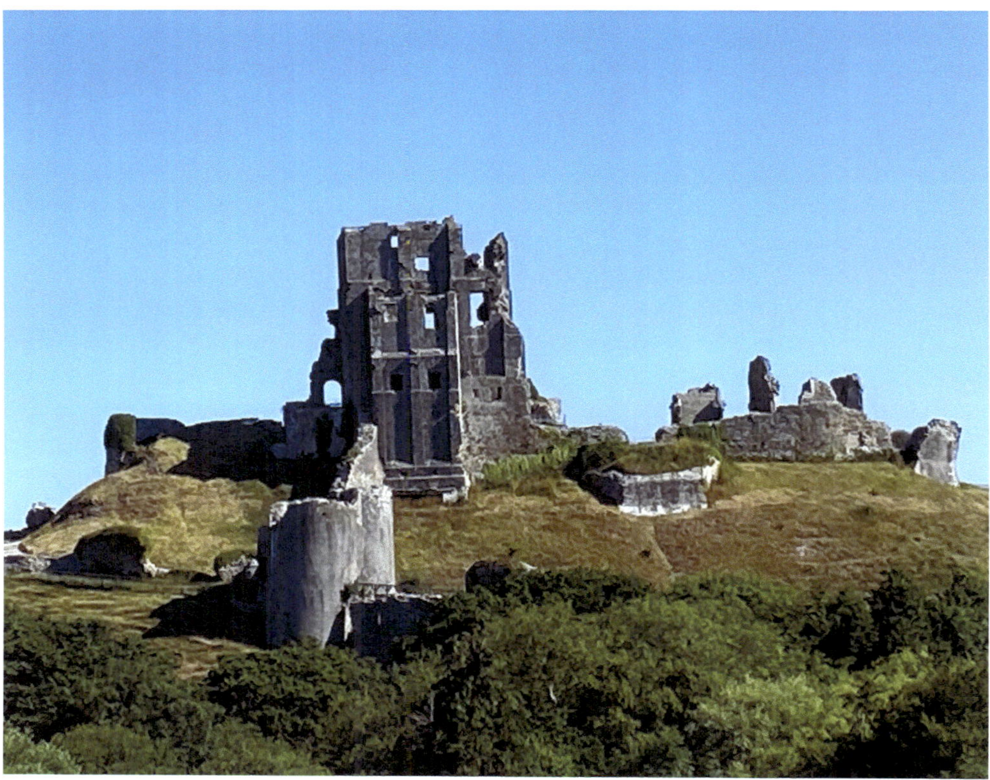

Corfe Castle.

further Viking marauders, after he had defeated the Danes at Peveril Point in AD 877 (see Chapter 2: Little London by the Sea).

Almost a hundred years later, the castle's gruesome early history involved the murder of Edward, the Saxon king and martyr (r. 975–978), when he visited Corfe Castle on 18 March 978. His father, King Edgar (r. 959–975), had died suddenly, precipitating a feud between the supporters of rival factions for the throne. The two potential candidates were the teenage Edward and his younger half-brother, Ethelred. However, it was Edward who received the crown, much to the chagrin of his stepmother, Elfrida, his father's second wife, who was keen to put her own son, Ethelred, on the throne and had plotted to do so for years.

Elfrida couldn't believe her luck when Edward, who had been hunting in the Isle of Purbeck, which in Saxon times was a royal chase preserved for hunting, became separated from the rest of the hunting party and decided to visit his brother, Ethelred, and his stepmother at Corfe Castle. Accordingly, the fifteen-year-old king arrived on horseback alone, and was welcomed with a goblet of wine. He was just enjoying his first few sips, still astride the horse, when he was stabbed by an assassin on the orders of his wicked stepmother. The horse bolted and dragged along Edwards's lifeless body, with his foot still stuck in the stirrups, before finally dislodging him into a stream.

Legend has it that a poor blind woman found the body and took it to her cottage nearby, where she covered it with rough clothing. Later in the night, the cottage was filled with a bright celestial light, and the woman's sight was restored. It is also said that in the thirteenth century, the Church of St Edward the Martyr was built where the old lady's cottage was situated.

Another aspect of the tale insists that Elfrida's servants found the body and on the orders of Elfrida flung it in a well. It is said that shortly afterwards, a ray of heavenly light illuminated the well and that the water received miraculous healing properties, resulting in the well-being known henceforth as St Edward's Fountain.

It is believed that Edward was initially buried with a distinct lack of ceremony at Lady St Mary Church, Wareham, but that the occurrence of further miracles at this site caused him to become recognised as a saint and martyr and resulted in his canonisation by the pope. His remains were hence removed to Shaftsbury Abbey, where they were given a burial more fit for a king and saint and this site also became a place of pilgrimage.

Another part of the legend asserts that Elfrida tried to deflect rumours regarding her part in the king's death and attempted to follow the funeral procession in an outward display of grief. However, karma was satisfied as she was suitably humiliated when her nag refused to move and instead she had to follow on foot. It is said that after that, she spent the remainder of her life in various nunneries in an attempt to repent for her sins.

Shaftsbury Abbey was destroyed in Henry VIII's (r. 1509–1547) Dissolution of the Monasteries in 1539, but the bones of the saint were hidden and avoided desecration. Many years later in 1931, the remains were found during archaeological excavation and the relics were donated to the St Edward the Martyr Orthodox Church in Woking, Surrey.

After Edward's death, Elfrida got her wish and her son was duly placed on the throne as Ethelred II (r. 978–1016). He was aged only ten when he acceded to the throne. He was badly advised and as a result was better known as Ethelred the Unready.

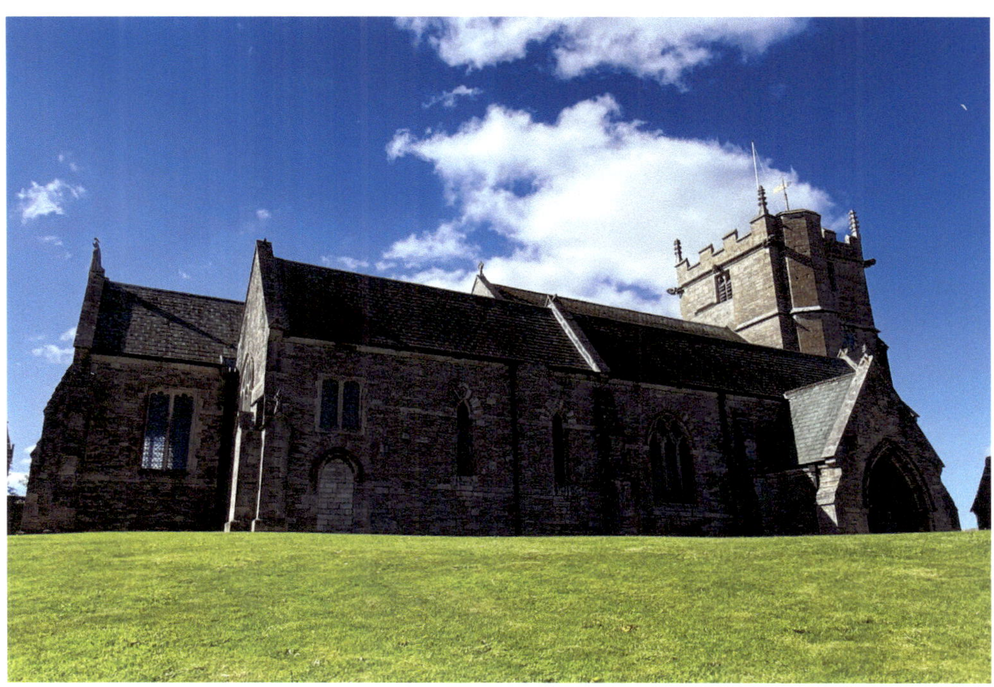

St Edward the Martyr Church, Corfe Castle.

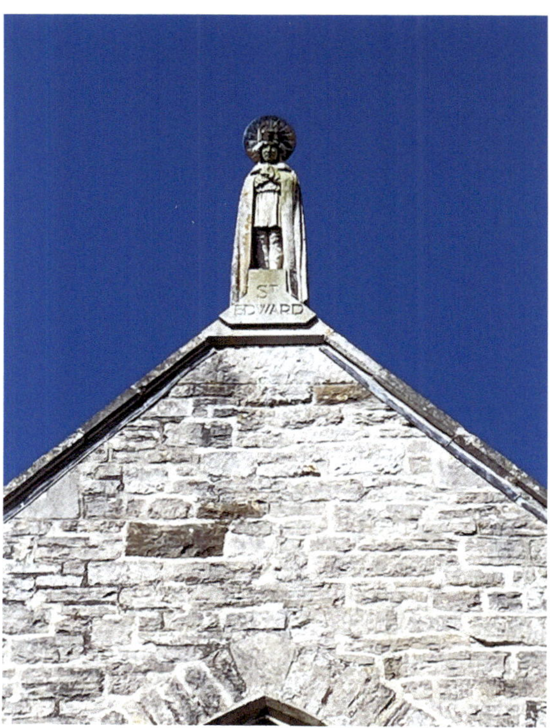

A statue of St Edward the Martyr on top of the St Edward the Martyr Church, Corfe Castle.

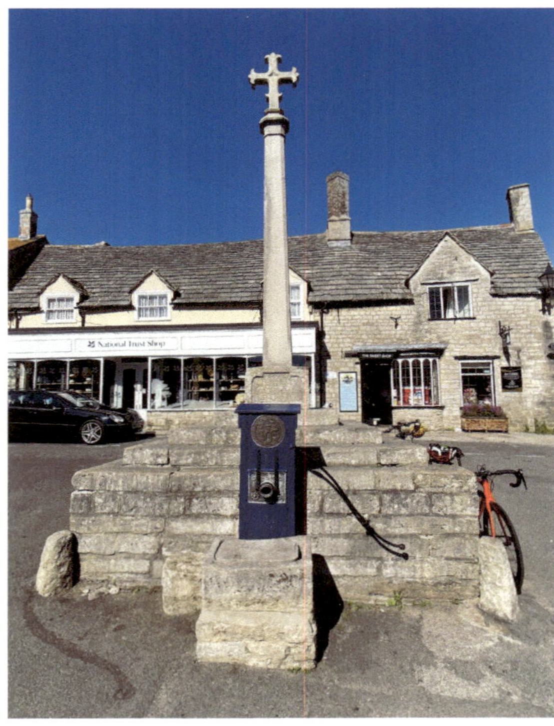

The Town Pump by the Market Cross bears the seal of Corfe Castle and is reputed to be situated above the well where the body of St Edward the Martyr was said to be hidden after his murder in AD 978.

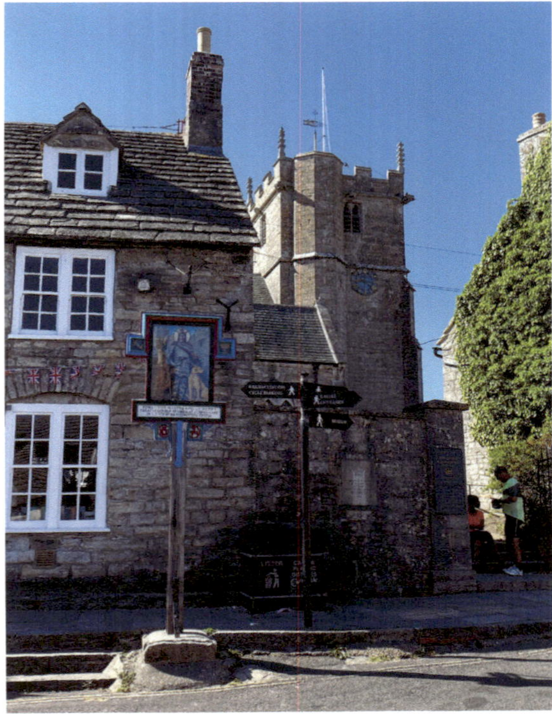

The tragedy of St Edward the Martyr is commemorated in the village 'Sign of four'.

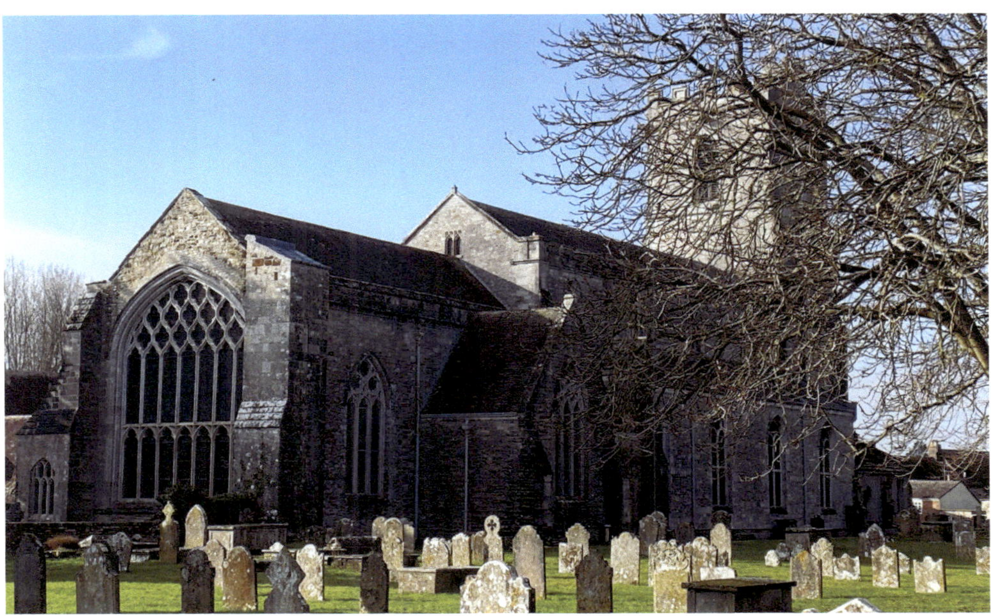

Lady St Mary Church, Wareham.

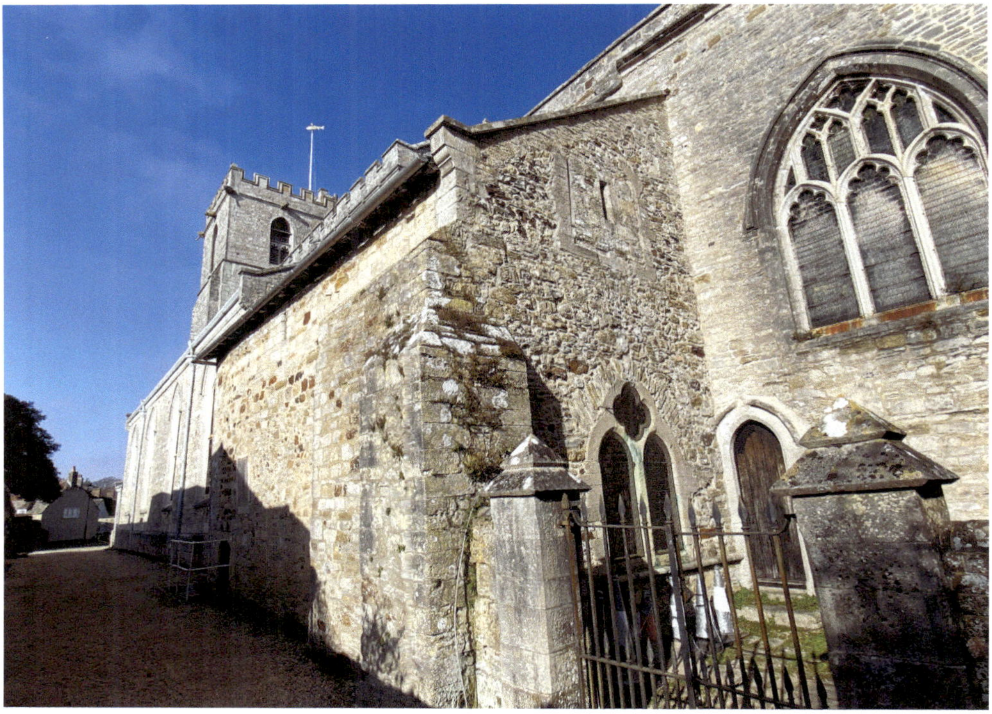

A tomb that is said to have once contained St Edward the Martyr when he was buried within Lady St Mary Church, Wareham, is situated in an early twelfth-century side chapel dedicated to the saint.

A constant feature of Ethelred's reign was the persistent marauding, raping and pillaging of England's coastline by the Vikings. Indeed in Dorset, only Corfe Castle remained unravaged. One of Ethelred's many mistakes was to pay the Viking Danes what was called 'Danegeld', which was a princely sum of money to stop them attacking England, which of course didn't work and only served to encourage them. The coins were minted in Wareham, which was considered an important enough settlement at the time to boast two mints.

Ethelred was succeeded by King Edmund Ironside (r. 1016–1017), who led the Saxons to defeat against the Danes at the Battle of Assandun in 1016, resulting in a subsequent treaty with the Danish King Cnut, who became King of England (r. 1017–1035).

Shortly after the Norman Conquest of 1066, William the Conqueror (1066–1087) organised the construction of castles the length and breadth of the country. They included Dover, the Tower of London, Arundel, Corfe Castle and Exeter. They were built as symbols of Norman power to control the populace. William particularly recognised the defensive capabilities of the site at Corfe and also took into account that it was close to the town of Wareham, which was an important port at the time. William was responsible for the building of the basic motte-and-bailey structure and developed it into an impregnable fortress of Purbeck limestone and a formidable symbol of Norman supremacy. The fact that the inner wall was constructed of stone, which was unusual in the eleventh century as the majority of castles in England were built from earth and timber during this period, indicates the high status of the castle as one of the most significant royal strongholds in the land.

Upon William's death in 1087, his three sons, Robert, William Rufus and Henry, were at loggerheads as they jockeyed for the throne. William's will granted the crown to William Rufus, rather than to his older son Robert, who instead was given the Duchy of Normandy. William Rufus (r. 1087–1100), met a suspicious death in the New Forest by virtue of an arrow in his back whilst he was hunting. Henry then crowned himself as King Henry I (r. 1100–1135) with indecent haste. As a result, he immediately found himself in conflict with his older brother, Robert, who he defeated at the Battle of Tinchebray (1106), enabling him to include Normandy as a possession of the English Crown. Robert was duly imprisoned in the large stone keep at Corfe Castle in 1107, which along with other improvements and further consolidation of fortifications was instigated by Henry. Robert was then moved to Devizes Castle where he spent the next twenty years, before finally being moved to Cardiff Castle, where he spent his final years.

DID YOU KNOW?
The walls of the keep are up to 10 feet thick.

Henry's son and heir, William, drowned in a shipwreck off Barfleur, France, in 1120, so shortly after Henry's death, the Anarchy (1135–1153) ensued, which was a civil war in which both Stephen, who had assumed the role of king (r. 1135–1154), and who was the son of William the Conquerors daughter, and Matilda, who was the daughter of Henry I, fought for the crown.

Corfe Castle found itself in the thick of the action as Baldwin de Redvers, Earl of Devon and a supporter of Matilda, ensconced himself in the royal stronghold with his garrison. An outraged King Stephen made haste from Exeter to besiege the castle, which proved impregnable to his forces, despite the fact that the besiegers built a ring and bailey castle nearby as a base from which to attack the fortress (the remaining earthworks can still be seen today).

The Anarchy eventually came to an end when an arrangement was brokered whereby Stephen would remain king until his death to be succeeded by Matilda's son, who became Henry II (r. 1154–1189).

Richard and John were the only two of King Henry II's eight sons who survived him and upon Henry's death Richard I (r. 1189–1199) was duly crowned. He spent the majority of his time on the crusade in the Holy Lands and while he was away, his brother managed affairs at home with his associate William Longchamp. Throughout this time, it is thought that John plotted against his brother.

In 1199, Richard I (the Lionheart) was killed by an arrow during a siege in France and John (r. 1199–1216), one of the most reviled monarchs of England, finally came to power.

Immediately on receiving the crown, he set about dealing with a potential threat to the throne in the form of his nephew, Prince Arthur of Brittany, who was the son of his deceased brother Geoffrey. John led an army to Poitou in France and captured the fifteen-year-old Arthur after besieging his fortress, the castle of Mirabeau. Some sources suggest Arthur was guarded at the Chateau de Falaise by Hubert de Burgh, who was ordered by King John to castrate and blind the prisoner. Hubert refused to comply with this brutal and malicious order, so King John personally tied a heavy weight to Arthur's body and dropped him into the River Seine and drowned him.

Another potential threat to the throne, Arthur's sister and John's niece, Eleanor, the Maid of Brittany, was also taken prisoner along with twenty-five French knights and brought back to Corfe Castle. Eleanor was well treated and had King William of Scotland's daughters, who were also John's prisoners, to share her captivity with. Eleanor was imprisoned in Corfe until 1222, before spending further periods of captivity at Gloucester, Marlborough and Bristol, where she died.

Corfe became John's favourite castle and he visited frequently. He particularly liked the dungeon facilities and found them ideal places in which to leave his prisoners to starve to death.

DID YOU KNOW?
The unfortunate French knights died in an oubliette, a particularly nasty dungeon. It means forget in French. The prisoners were thrown through a trap door into a windowless pit and just left to starve to death.

John liked the castle so much that he had a new luxury royal residence built next to the keep, which was called the Gloriette and was where he kept his crown jewels.

DID YOU KNOW?
A trebuchet is a type of catapult. In 1216, King John brought one to the castle along with a battering ram and there is a mock-up of one now within the castle grounds.

King John managed to lose most of England's lands in France, earning him the moniker of 'Lackland'. As a result of this and due to Corfe Castle's proximity to the south coast, he had the defences strengthened and the work continued for ten years. He was also at loggerheads with his barons who forced him to sign the Magna Carta, enshrining the rights of free men in 1215. However, as soon as he has regained sufficient power to resist the barons, he renounced the charter and was consequently at war with them again.

DID YOU KNOW?
A garderobe was the term used to describe a medieval toilet. Among King John's servants many unenviable jobs was the task of making sure that the garderobe was in a suitable state for the king to patronage. However, yet another aspect of a royal servant's life that was distinctly unpleasant was that their quarters were shared with flea-ridden dogs, which caused the servant's clothes to also become infested. Still happily, this problem was solved by hanging the clothes in the garderobe overnight and allowing the putrid smell to kill the fleas. This practice is where the term wardrobe has arisen from.

Another unpleasant story involving King John led to a stretch of the Wareham Walls becoming known as the Bloody Bank, when in 1213 a hermit by the name of Peter de Pomfret was dragged here tied to a horse's tail and then hanged for predicting that King John's reign would come to a premature end.

DID YOU KNOW?
The grisly reputation of the Bloody Bank at Wareham was further enhanced 472 years later in 1685 when five Monmouth rebels from the Protestant rebellion against the Catholic King James II (r. 1685–1688) were hanged, drawn and

quartered here after being sentenced by the 'Hanging Judge', Judge Jeffreys, at the Bloody Assizes in Dorchester. So many prisoners were convicted of High Treason after the failed Monmouth Rebellion (1685), which had culminated at the Battle of Sedgemoor (1685), the last pitched battle to occur on English soil, that the executioners complained that they could only cope with thirteen hanging, drawing and quarterings a day, as the process was so time consuming. As a result, gallows were also erected at Bridport, Weymouth, Poole and Wareham, as the condemned were farmed out in batches to the various locations.

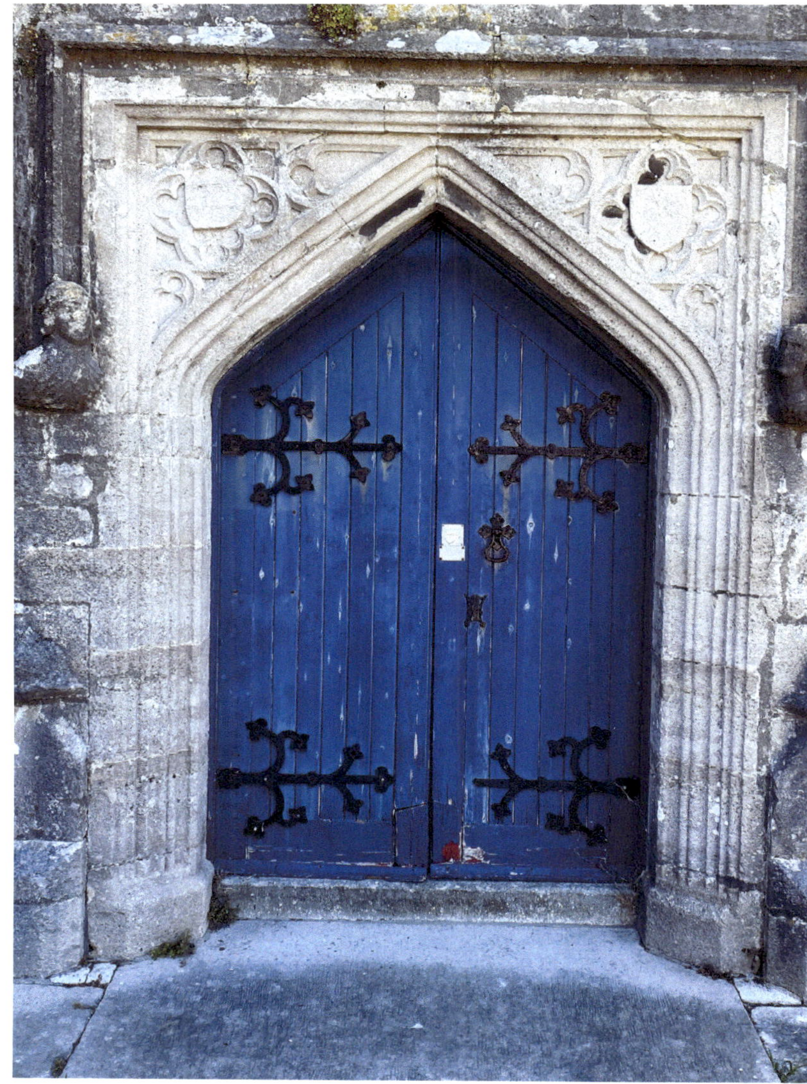

The back door of St Edward the Martyr Church, Corfe Castle. The fact that one of the shields is set on its side is said to intonate the illegitimacy of King John.

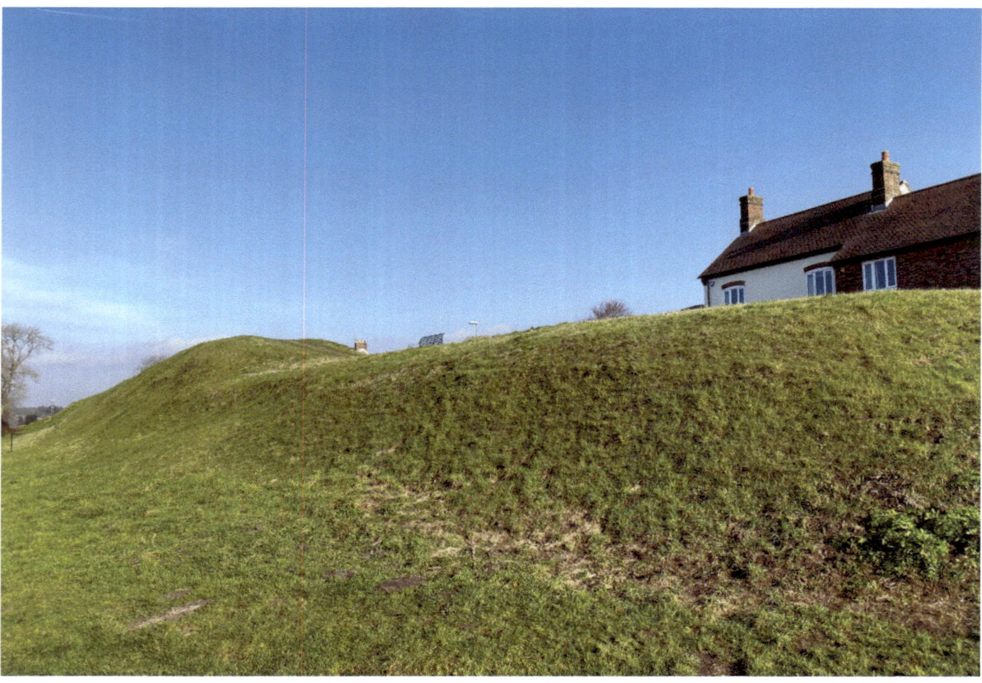

The Bloody Bank – Wareham Walls.

King John's son, Henry III (r. 1216–1272), was only nine on the death of his father, and his ascension came in the middle of what was known as the First Baron's War (1215–1217). However, his forces managed to regain royal sovereignty from the barons after victories at Lincoln and Sandwich, both in 1217.

In 1221, Henry ousted the powerful baron Peter de Mauley from his position of Constable of Corfe Castle and had him imprisoned. But in 1230, Peter de Mauley was back in favour and regained his post. Then, the barons led by Simon de Montfort rebelled again and defeated Henry at the Battle of Lewes (1264) and subsequently regained Corfe Castle. However, in 1265, King Henry's son, Prince Edward, defeated de Montfort at the Battle of Evesham (1265) and Corfe Castle was once again in royal hands.

In 1272, Prince Edward became King Edward I (r. 1272–1307) and he wasted no time in turning Corfe Castle into an even more formidable stronghold by improving the defences of both the outer and south-west gatehouses. Then in 1275, he captured his nemesis' Simon de Montfort's son and imprisoned him at Corfe Castle.

Edward II (r. 1307–1327) came to the throne and was very different to his warmongering father. His army was defeated at the Battle of Banockburn (1314) by the Scots, resulting in Scotland becoming an independent kingdom again. Edward II's wife and Roger Mortimer then plotted to depose the king and had him imprisoned at Corfe Castle briefly, before he was transferred to Berkeley Castle where he was tortured with unspeakable cruelty, before meeting a very unpleasant death, whereby, according to one source, he was blinded by a red-hot poker which was then inserted into his anus.

From 1356, Edward II's son, King Edward III (r. 1327–1377), carried out a programme of repairs to the castle, which continued for twenty years, then in 1461, King Edward IV (r. 1461–1483) ascended to the throne and handed the castle to his youngest brother, the future King Richard III (r. 1483–1485).

In 1496, King Henry VII (r. 1485–1509) moved his mother, Lady Margaret Beaufort, Countess of Richmond, into the castle. However, the castle reverted back to being Crown property on the death of Lady Margaret in 1509. It then remained in royal ownership until Queen Elizabeth I (r. 1558–1603) sold it to one of her favourites, Christopher Hatton, in 1571. The castle was then passed down in the family to Sir Christopher's nephew, William, and then William's wife, Elizabeth, who in turn sold it to the Attorney General Sir John Bankes in 1635.

The English Civil War (1642–1652) pitted the Royalist supporters of King Charles I (r. 1625–1649) against the Parliamentarians led by Oliver Cromwell (r. 1653–1658). At the outbreak of the conflict, the majority of English people supported the institution of the monarchy, but the issue was whether the monarchy or parliament had ultimate power. Those who supported Charles I in his claim of the 'Divine Right of Kings' and the monarch's superiority over parliament were known as Royalists, while their Parliamentarian opponents were in favour of a constitutional monarchy.

Sir John and Mary Bankes were staunch Royalists and Sir John spent most of his time in attendance of the king in his role as Attorney General. As a result John was absent from the castle on royal business, initially in York and then in Oxford, when civil war broke out, which left Mary with a handful of women and five men to defend the castle, where she lived with her children.

Initially, the Royalists enjoyed great success, securing victory at the Battle of Edgehill (1642), which put the Parliamentarians on the back foot. However, in 1643 the Covenanter Scots, led by Archibald Campbell, 9th Earl of Argyll, chief of the powerful Clan Campbell, advocated civil and religious union with England as the best way to preserve a Presbyterian Kirk. They made an agreement called the Solemn League and Covenant, in which the Scottish Covenanters agreed to offer military support to the English Parliamentarians. As a result, the Civil War started to turn in favour of the Parliamentarians and by 1643, Mary was expecting trouble, as by now almost all of Dorset was under Parliamentary control and Corfe Castle was the last remaining Royalist stronghold in south-west England. Also, Sir John had been declared a traitor by the Parliamentarians and his estates had been ordered to be confiscated. Rumours abounded that the Parliamentarians were intending to strike whilst the Purbeck men were enjoying the traditional May Day stag hunt, and consequently Mary mounted some cannons on the outer bailey and ordered her supporters inside and locked the gates.

Sure enough, on 23 June 1643, the Parliamentarians did make their first attempt to capture the castle and it was laid siege to by about 500 men. The Parliamentarians tried unsuccessfully to gain entry with cannon and scaling ladders and they also tried to smash their way in with two battering rams known as the 'Sow and the Boar'. Each attack was repelled by the inhabitants, who launched heavy stones and burning coals at the defenders from the fortified barricades. The besiegers summoned the castle to surrender, but it was to no avail, so instead they took the village. In this way they prevented provisions coming into the castle and also threatened to burn down the Bankes' tenant's homes in the village unless Mary Bankes removed her four cannons, which she duly did, after a ceasefire was arranged for the besieged to reprovision.

During the ceasefire period, Captain Lawrence, along with eighty soldiers from a local Royalist unit, arrived to add support and with their help the castle continued to hold out against the Parliamentarians for a further six weeks, until news reached the Parliamentarians that more Royalist support was on its way causing them to beat a hasty retreat.

The Parliamentarians had lost a hundred men in the action, whereas the Royalists only lost two. It seemed as though the Parliamentarians had missed a gilt-edge opportunity and indeed they didn't get to have another crack at the castle until 1646.

After the first siege, Sir John Bankes was reunited with Lady Bankes and they produced a son, William, who was born at Corfe Castle in June 1644. However, Sir John died shortly afterwards in Oxford in December 1644.

The combined force of English Parliamentarians and Scottish Covenanters then went on to win a series of battles during 1644, and, most significantly, the Battle of Marston Moor on 2 July of that year. Another factor in the Parliamentarians' success was the founding of the first professional army in England, known as the New Model Army, which led to further success at the Battle of Naseby (1645).

The Parliamentarians were now very much in the ascendancy, so they turned their attention again to Corfe Castle, which continued to be the only Royalist castle still holding out between Exeter and London. This time they arrived with more men and more military hardware than the first siege. However as before, the castle continued to withstand the onslaught, despite the Parliamentarians setting up cannon emplacements in the nearby church of St Edward the Martyr and the Rings, which were the remains of a fortification originally built by Stephen to attack the castle during the Anarchy.

However, the heavy bombardment and the starvation conditions were beginning to take its toll on the besieged and after seven weeks loyalty was beginning to waver in some quarters. Colonel Pitman left the castle on the pretence that he was going to return with Royalist reinforcements. Instead, he secretly made a deal with Colonel Bingham, the Parliamentarian commander, and returned under the cover of darkness on 27 February 1646 with 120 Parliamentarian troops from nearby Lulworth Castle. They were disguised as Royalists and thus gained entrance to the castle and occupied the stronghold from within, which in turn forced Lady Bankes to surrender, finally putting an end to the siege.

The Parliamentarians allowed Lady Bankes and her garrison to leave unharmed and Lady Bankes was ceremoniously presented with the castle keys in recognition of her bravery. The keys were only of sentimental value though, as shortly after the castle's capture, senior figures from the town of Poole petitioned Parliament to demolish the castle and fine Lady Bankes, so that soldiers and poor inhabitants of Poole and other towns in the county who had supported Parliament could receive some compensation for the hardship they had suffered during the Civil War.

Poole had supported the Parliamentarians, mainly because the wealthy merchants who had become rich due to the trade with Newfoundland were against the ship money tax imposed by Charles I and were also not very happy with the lack of protection from pirates afforded by the Crown. Parliament subsequently ordered the demolition of the castle and a team of sappers (engineers) set about destroying it with the aid of gunpowder, hence the state we see it in today. However, the destruction of Corfe Castle did have one bonus for the villagers in that it provided a readymade supply of building material and even today some houses in the village still possess this original stone.

Cromwell died on 3 September 1658 and was succeeded by his son, Richard, who soon found himself unsuited for government. A chaotic period ensued during which he was unable to control the warring factions of the army and Parliament. In May 1659 he was ordered to resign by the army and Prince Charles I's exiled son was then invited by Parliament to ascend the throne as Charles II (r. 1660–1685). To mark the event, the royal arms of King Charles II was painted on a wooden board above a thirteenth-century window from the north aisle of St Edward the Martyr Church.

After the restoration of the monarchy, the Bankes family rose again and Lady Bankes' son Ralph built a new mansion on land acquired by Sir John in the 1630s, at Kingston Lacy. The stately home near Wimborne is where the family still reside today.

After a period of confiscation, the castle was returned to the Bankes family, who retained it within the family until 1982, when Sir Ralph Bankes, a direct descendant of Sir John Bankes, bequeathed the whole of the Bankes Estate to the National Trust, including Corfe Castle and Kingston Lacy, making it still the largest donation ever bequeathed to the National Trust.

There are two pubs in the locality using the name of Bankes, one being the Bankes Arms Hotel, Corfe Castle, the other being the Bankes Arms Inn at Studland.

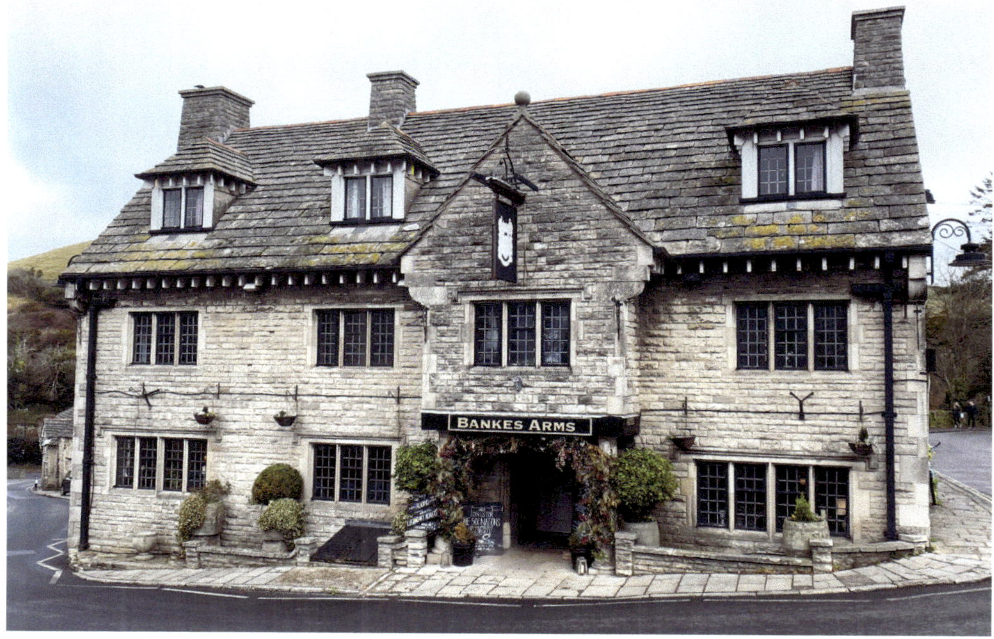

The Bankes Arms in the village of Corfe Castle is a Grade II listed manor house with a bar and a restaurant. The building dates back to 1549, almost a century before the siege.

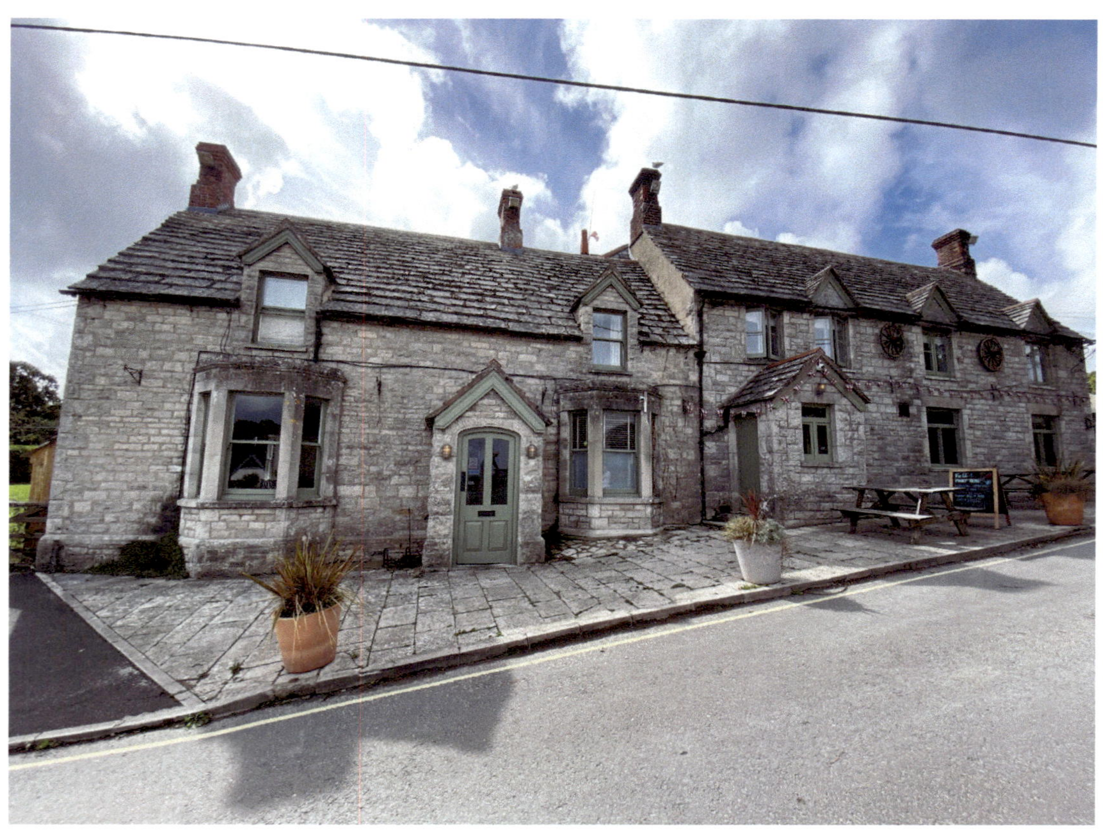

The Bankes Arms Inn in Studland dates back to the sixteenth century and is built from locally quarried stone. It has its own brewery and is an old smugglers haunt.

4. Smuggling in Swanage and the Purbecks

By the late seventeenth century, piracy was abating, but a new unlawful trade of smuggling was becoming widespread and in the sixteenth, seventeenth, eighteenth and nineteenth centuries, peaking between 1770 and 1815, many coastlines abounded with smugglers. There were mitigating factors to these activities, as it was a time when high taxes were sought to finance wars. Also the imposition of duty on imported goods significantly raised prices beyond the pocket of most people and for many on the Swanage and Purbeck coastline, smuggling was a way of life.

The contraband consisted mainly of tobacco, wine and tea, for which there was always a great demand, and many of the gang leaders became very wealthy on the proceeds. However, by the 1850s, the effect of the return of peace after the Napoleonic Wars, along with more efficient customs and tax reductions, all but destroyed the practice.

Another factor in the decline of smuggling was the introduction of the coast guard in the 1820's, which increased the risk of being caught. HM Coastguard was formed by combining the Preventative Water Guard, Riding Officers and Customs Officers and its main role was to combat smuggling. The main weapon at their disposal locally was an armed cutter which patrolled the sea between Portland and the Isle of Wight.

In the Purbeck area, the most prolific smuggler was Isaac Gulliver (1745–1822), who, along with the army of people working for him, was responsible for a vast amount of illicit goods arriving from the sea. He was the son of a smuggler and inevitably he married into a smuggling family. He was Dorset's most celebrated and successful smuggler – although he was actually born in Wiltshire.

In the late 1770s, he moved from Wiltshire to the White Hart public house at Longham and then to West Howe House in Kinson, now in the Borough of Bournemouth, but in those days part of Poole. He controlled a massive smuggling operation which spread its tentacles across the whole of Dorset, Devon, Wiltshire and Hampshire. He even had the brassneck to provide his men with a kind of smuggling uniform which consisted of smocks and whitened hair; hence their nickname the 'white wigs'.

He became a wanted man after his involvement in a clash with customs officers between Bournemouth and Poole. However, he regularly evaded their attention, and on one occasion was secreted out of the King's Head in Poole, hidden inside a barrel, under the very noses of customs officials. On another occasion, he eluded customs men by lying motionless in a coffin with his face covered with white powder as he played dead.

Of course, it didn't go unnoticed to Gulliver that the Purbeck coastline in the vicinity of Swanage particularly lent itself to smuggling, and to take advantage of this situation, Gulliver is said to have made a cottage beside the Post Office in Worth Matravers his home for a period in the 1700s, when he turned the village into a command centre for many local smuggling operations as he plied his nefarious trade along the rugged coastline.

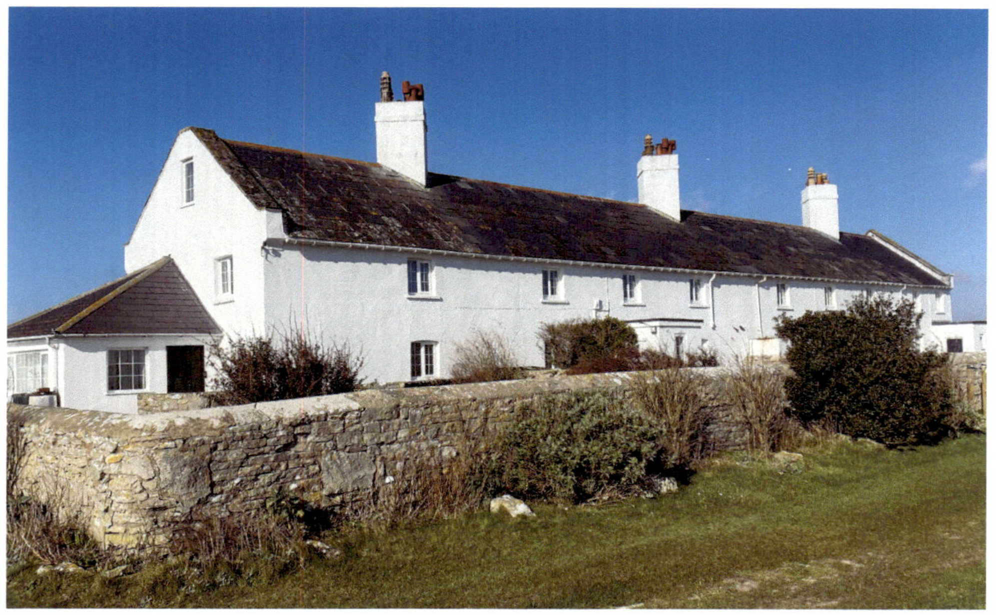

Coastguard cottages – St Aldhelm's Head.

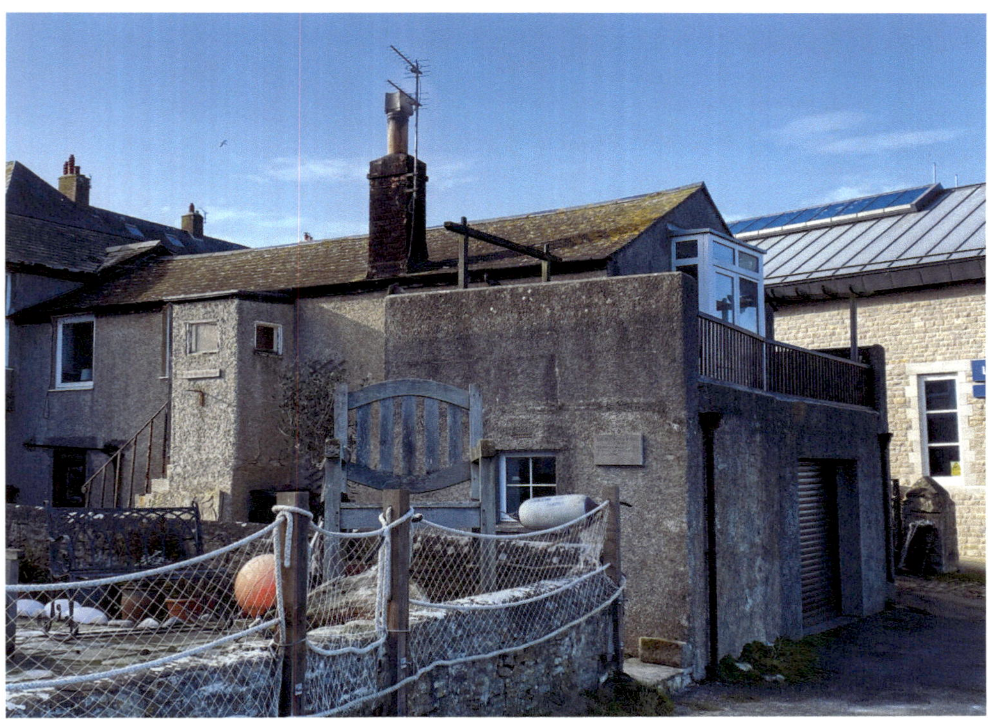

The Watch House, Swanage. Built in 1827, the watch was situated here for the prevention of smuggling.

He had a fleet of fifteen luggers, from which his men would unload the contraband on the coastline. What couldn't be transported immediately was concealed. The rest was transported with the aid of packhorses to holding areas, before it was distributed by his fleet of horse-drawn wagons as far afield as the Midlands, London, Bristol and Bath.

The steep cliffs and the nature of this treacherous coastline restricted the amount of suitable places that contraband could be landed between Durlston Head and St Aldhelm's Head, so the main possibilities were the quarries at Tilly Whim, Dancing Ledge, Hedbury Seacombe and Winspit, as all five had sea platforms for lowering stone onto boats. However, once the smuggled goods were ashore, the spectacular coastline was a smuggler's dream, providing numerous hidden coves and tunnels suitable for the purposes of the concealing of the illegal imports.

Another factor was that many of the smugglers were also quarrymen, so they had reason to be hanging around at the landing stages. It was also said that many quarry workers carried their lunch to work in a rush basket, which then had the secondary use at the end of the day for bringing back contraband from adjacent caves close to the quarries where they worked.

The quarrymen involved in the trade were also familiar with the numerous tunnels under the cliffs where contraband could be stored and it was said that the tunnels joined up and that it was possible to walk through them all the way to Swanage.

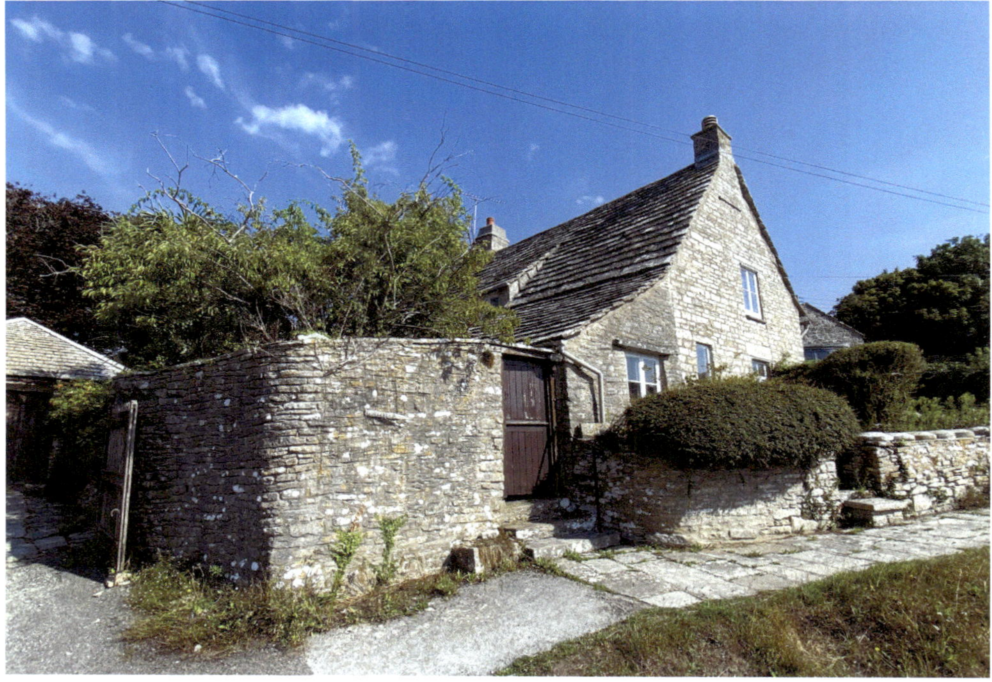

Gullivers's House, Worth Matravers. The house which overlooks the duck pond in Worth Matravers also has a good view out to sea, which enabled Gulliver's wife to act as a look-out for the boats bringing in the contraband from France.

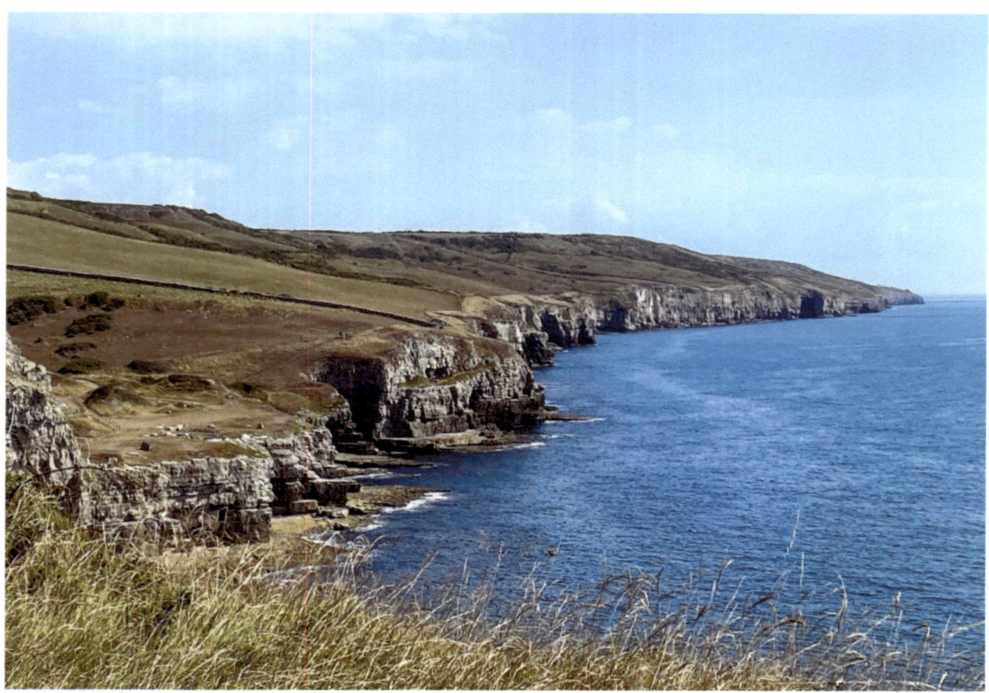

The coastline from Seacombe to Anvil Point. The Purbeck coast is riddled with caves – some formed naturally and some by quarrying. This allied to the landing stages used in the quarrying industry made the area a veritable smuggler's paradise.

The fact that some of the quarries were close to habitation and to coastguard stations didn't present too much of a problem, as the smugglers knew the coastguard's movements. Also the numerous stacks of stones and the number of men in the quarries made it difficult for the coastguard to identify stashes of contraband and which of the workers were also smugglers.

From Worth Matravers and Langton Matravers, the smugglers were very adept at navigating the treacherous rocky paths leading down to the coast. They also utilised the farmer's stone walls to help them feel their way in the darkness. The revenue men, on the other hand, weren't as familiar with the paths and they kept to the main tracks, which they marked with white washed stones. However, the smugglers got wise to this and removed the stones and placed them in such a fashion as to lead the revenue men over the cliff edge, resulting in some falling to their deaths in the dark.

DID YOU KNOW?
The smugglers referred to the coastguards as 'ring bums', as they sat and watched for long periods.

When unloading their boats, smugglers in the Purbeck area were often under severe pressure to avoid detection from customs officials. If it was suspected the coastguard were around, they wouldn't unload the goods on the shore and instead would 'seed the sea', which involved tying ropes to the barrels and throwing them overboard. The ropes had an iron bar at one end to ensure they stayed submerged and a cork attached to the other to enable the crew of a cutter to identify and retrieve the contraband at a later date.

One of Gulliver's holding areas was Spyway Barn, which still exists as a tourist information point owned by the National Trust and is a Grade II listed building. It is in the vicinity of Langton Matravers as you head towards Dancing Ledge.

Inevitably the barn has a colourful history and nineteenth-century local folklore recalls that the smugglers would often release a ferocious bull to terrorise the villagers, so that the authorities were kept busy trying to contain it, effectively keeping potential prying eyes away as contraband was being loaded. The smuggled goods were then moved from Spyway Barn further inland to St George's Church, Langton Matravers, where the goods were stored in the roof. Over time, as a result of this alternative use of church facilities, the whole structure became so severely weakened and unsafe that it was necessary to completely rebuild it.

The smuggling fraternity had a strict code of conduct and any disloyalty or treachery was severely punished with beatings or even hangings. There is a lone sycamore tree,

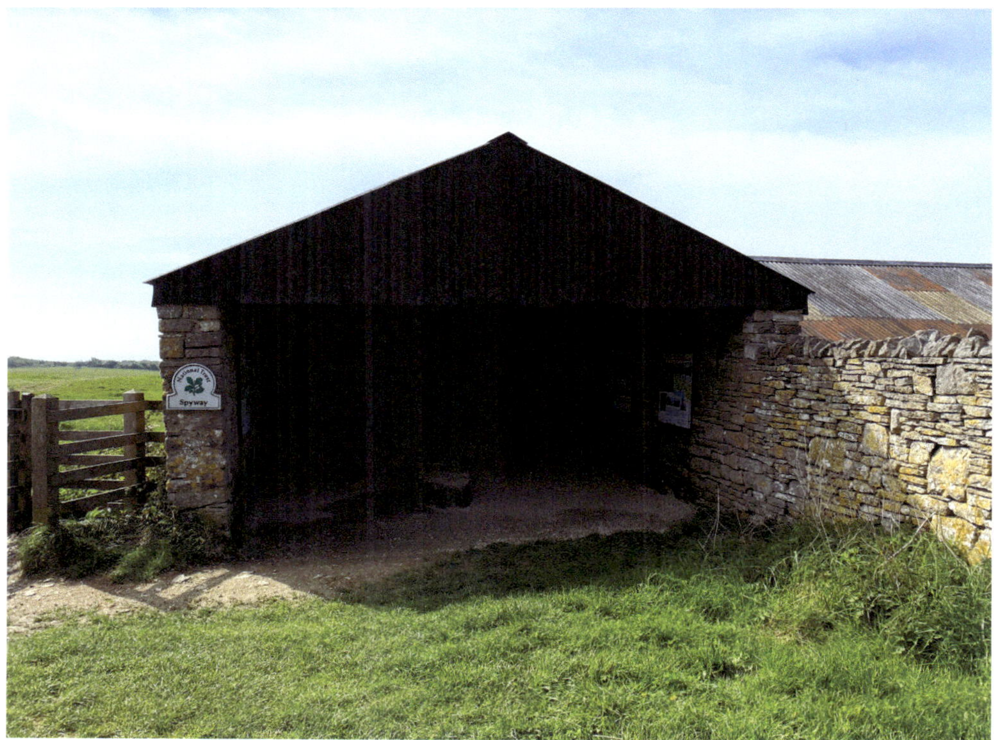

Spyway Barn.

which can still be seen near Spyway Barn, that is reputed to have been used as a hangman's tree. Possibly the victims were smugglers who had betrayed their fellows.

On one occasion a smuggler was suspected of disloyalty when customs men removed a large pile of stones to reveal one of Gulliver's large contraband stores. The smuggler in question escaped a lynching, as it was not known for sure who was responsible, but later that night, he had to endure the sight of a burning effigy outside his house as an intimidating warning.

Having amassed a tidy fortune, Gulliver eventually retired from smuggling, and was given a king's pardon by George III (r. 1760–1820). This was believed to have been because he discovered a plot to assassinate the monarch and alerted the authorities. A grateful George III is supposed to have said, 'Let Gulliver smuggle as much as he wants', which may explain how he was never caught and was able to smuggle with impunity. Others say it was because he was given a chance in 1784 to wipe the slate clean by providing two of his men for active service in the Royal Navy.

He then became a wine merchant (although it was believed that a large proportion of his wine was of the smuggled variety), banker, civic leader and churchwarden in Wimborne. He lived to a great age and upon his death was buried in the vault of Wimborne Minster. His legacy still lives on throughout Dorset and despite his powerful build and appearance, he was considered to be a gentleman. It is claimed his pistol, which now resides in the Russell Cotes Museum in Bournemouth, was never used.

At the Swanage end of Langton Matravers High Street is a pub which a lot of quarrymen frequented, some of whom welcomed the opportunity to supplement their meagre income with a little smuggling. As a result, many a barrel of smuggled French brandy was illicitly secreted into the premises in the dead of night. The pub in question is a Grade II listed building and a free house with a nice garden at the rear. It is unusual in that it also doubles up as the village shop, which was an innovation during the Covid times of 2020. It was originally called the Mason's Arms, when it first opened in 1743, before a change of name to the King's Arms, when patriotic fervour enveloped the country in response to a potential invasion by Napoleon's French forces in 1803. The pub still retains the authentic atmosphere of the quarryman's pub, with its stone flagged floors and Purbeck marble fireplace.

One of the most renowned smugglers of Langton Matravers was Charles Hayward, who was also a churchwarden and quarrymen at Dancing Ledge, a mile to the south of the village. He and his fellow smugglers were regulars at the Kings Arms and were in league with the landlord William Marshfield, who was only too happy to turn a blind eye to their extracurricular activities. He also assisted them in storing the contraband that had been transported from the quarry, hidden in horse-drawn wagons under a few tons of stone. Indeed on one occasion, Marshfield managed to foil customs men searching the premises, by concealing the illicit goods under the bed occupied by his wife as she endured the labour pains of childbirth.

In nearby Worth Matravers, the Square and Compass was another quarrymen's pub and the name and pub sign indicate the tools of that profession and are also the internationally recognised symbol of the Freemasons. Indeed the origins of that medieval fraternity are from the quarrying and stone masonry industry. The pub dates back to

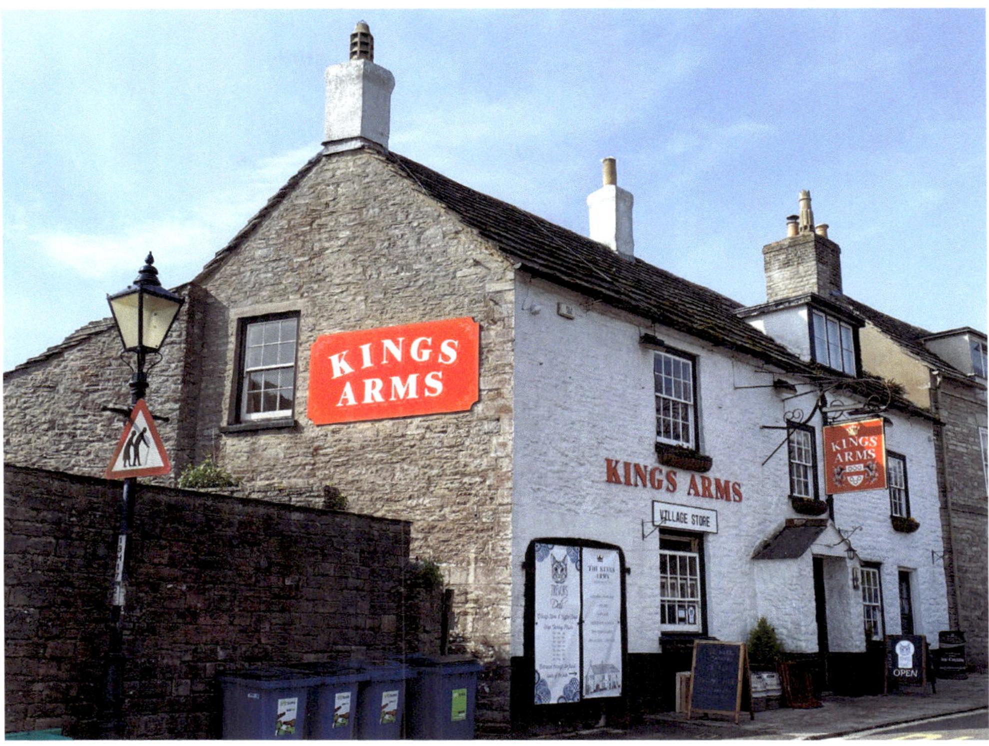

The King's Arms, Langton Matravers.

1752, but was two adjoining cottages prior to that. It also had a reputation as a smugglers pub and on one occasion, when a smuggler was injured in a skirmish with excise men at St Aldhelm's Head, he was carried by his fellow smugglers to the premises, where he later died of his wounds.

Chapman's Pool was another hidden cove which was ideal for smuggling, although the approach to the cove by sea from the west via Kimmeridge was notoriously dangerous and the smugglers referred to the Kimmeridge Ledges as 'Dead Man's Fingers', because of the numerous treacherous submerged rocks.

Another arch smuggler who was very active on the Swanage and Purbeck coast was a man named Lucas, who, with his gang, mainly operated around the St Aldhelm's Head area, where they landed the contraband before moving it inland. He was the landlord of the Ship Inn at Wool during the 1820s, so his main smuggling concern was French brandy. He was known to be an exceptionally violent man and his gang usually carried an assortment of deadly weapons, including pistols, swords, bludgeons, poles and flail type weapons called swingles.

His gang was involved in a clash with revenue men, which resulted in one smuggler being shot dead and many others wounded, as large quantities of brandy, gin and tea were confiscated by the revenue men. Later in 1827, another clash with revenue men resulted in the death of two coastguards. However, the coastguards on this occasion were

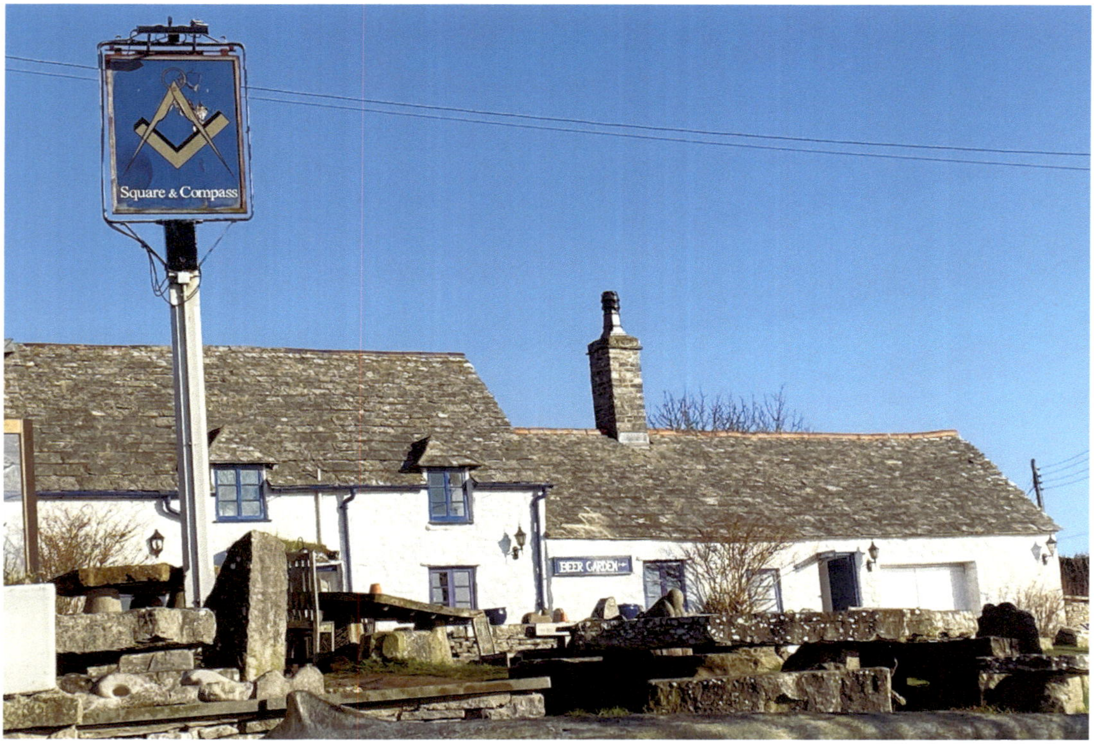

The Square and Compass, Worth Matravers.

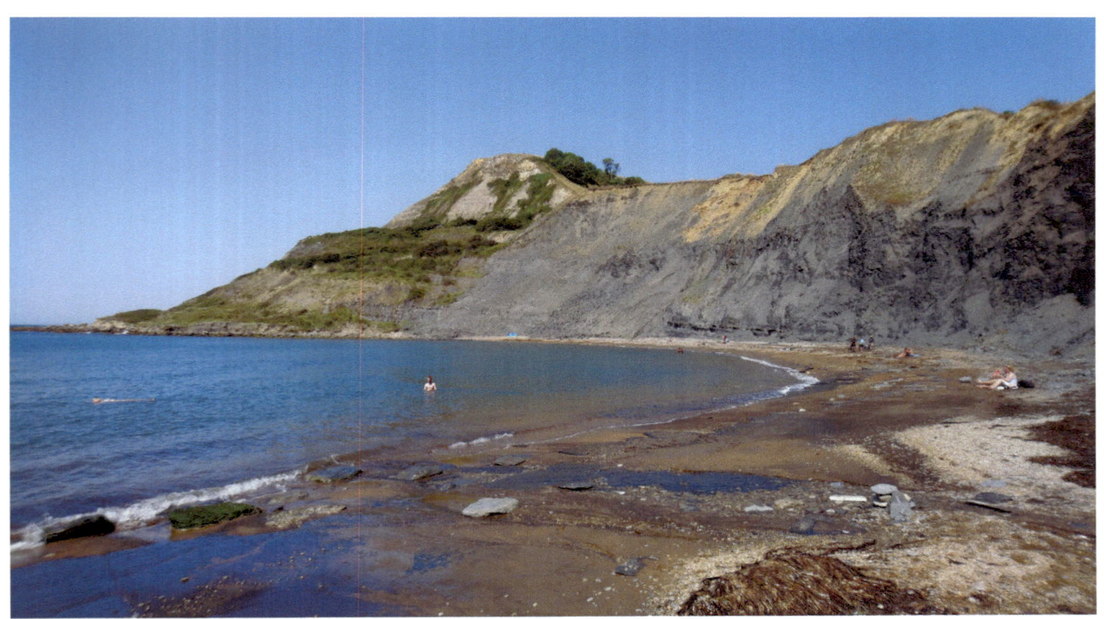

Chapman's Pool.

able to identify several of the smugglers including the ringleader, Lucas. He made his escape but was now a wanted man.

Captain Johnson soon discovered his name and learnt that he was the landlord of the Ship Inn. The next day customs men tricked their way into the pub, during a period in the day when it was shut. Captain Johnson mimicked a little girl's voice as she asked for some French brandy for her sick mother. Lucas opened the door and was promptly arrested and sent to Dorchester jail, where he served a long sentence and eventually died.

The smooth sandy bay of Studland was also conducive to smuggling and was ideal as the booty could be hidden amongst the sand dunes and then moved across the heathland.

There is a grave in St Nicholas' churchyard for Sergeant William Lawrence, who was involved in the Napoleonic Peninsular War and was at the Battle of Waterloo. However, his tombstone doesn't mention the fact that he also became the area's principal smuggler, after he became the landlord of a pub, appropriately called the Wellington Arms, situated opposite where the Bankes Arms Inn now stands. In fairness to him though, all of the other pub landlords in Studland were at it as well, including the landlord of what is now the only remaining pub in Studland – the Bankes Arms Inn.

Corfe Castle was also a place where many in the local community had a hand in smuggling and as elsewhere in the Purbecks many concerned with the quarrying and stone masonry industry were involved. They moved the contraband that had arrived from the coast in the dead of night and covered the horses' hooves and wagons with cloth, so that they could move soundlessly across Corfe Common.

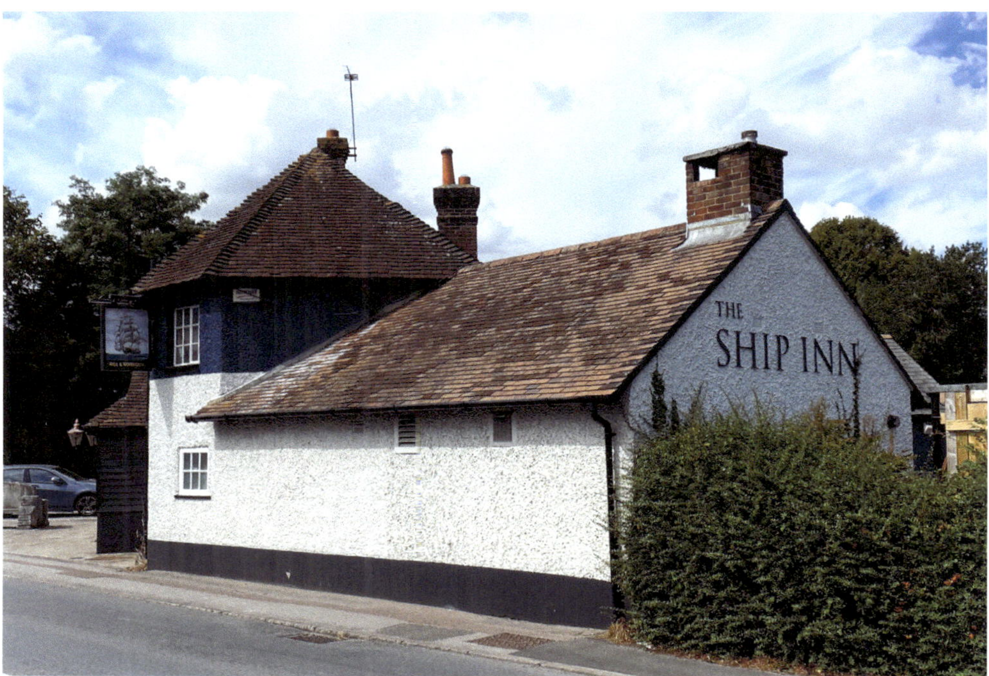

The Ship Inn, Wool.

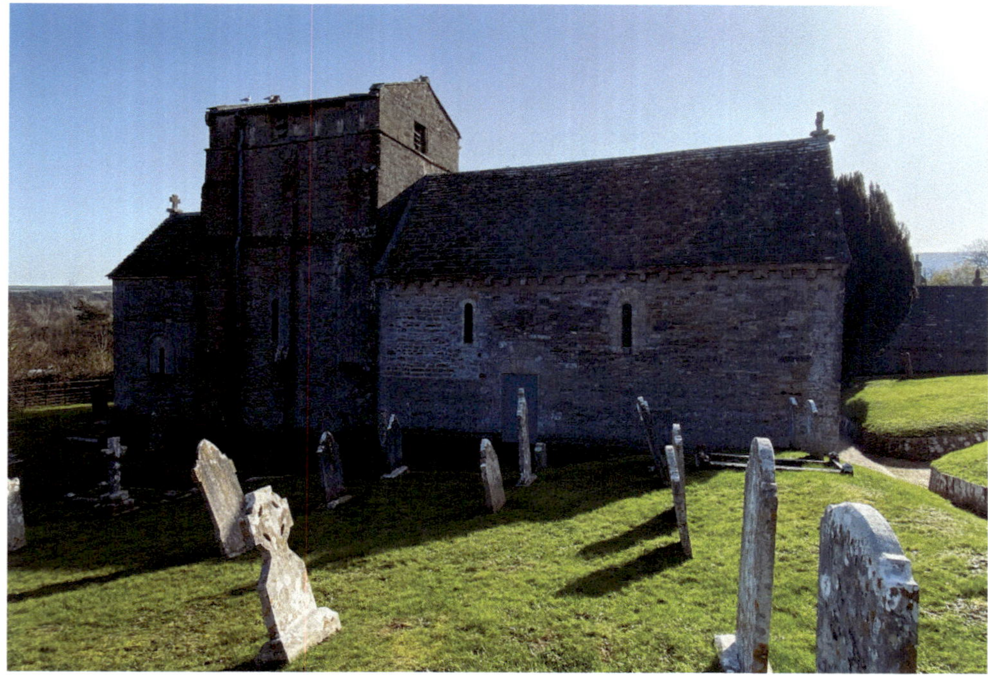

St Nicholas' Church, Studland.

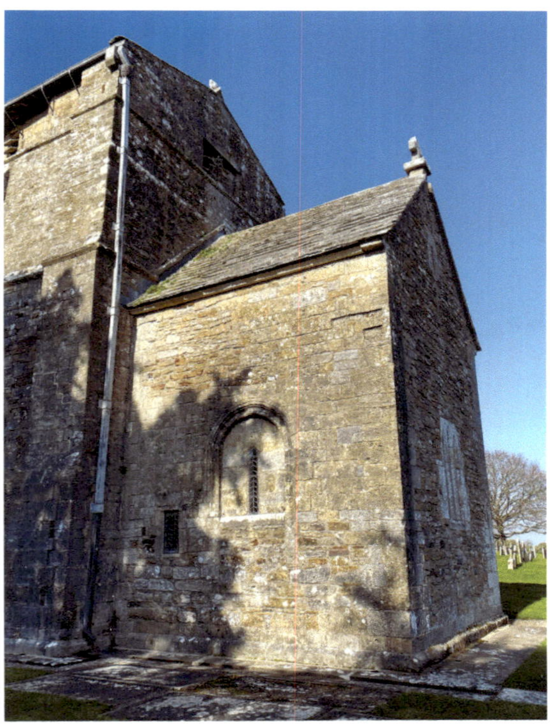

The smuggler's room above the sanctuary of St Nicholas' Church, Studland. During the sixteenth to eighteenth centuries the room above the sanctuary was used to store ill-gotten gains, initially from piracy and then from smuggling. The clergy turned a blind eye, as like most of the village they were complicit in the trade.

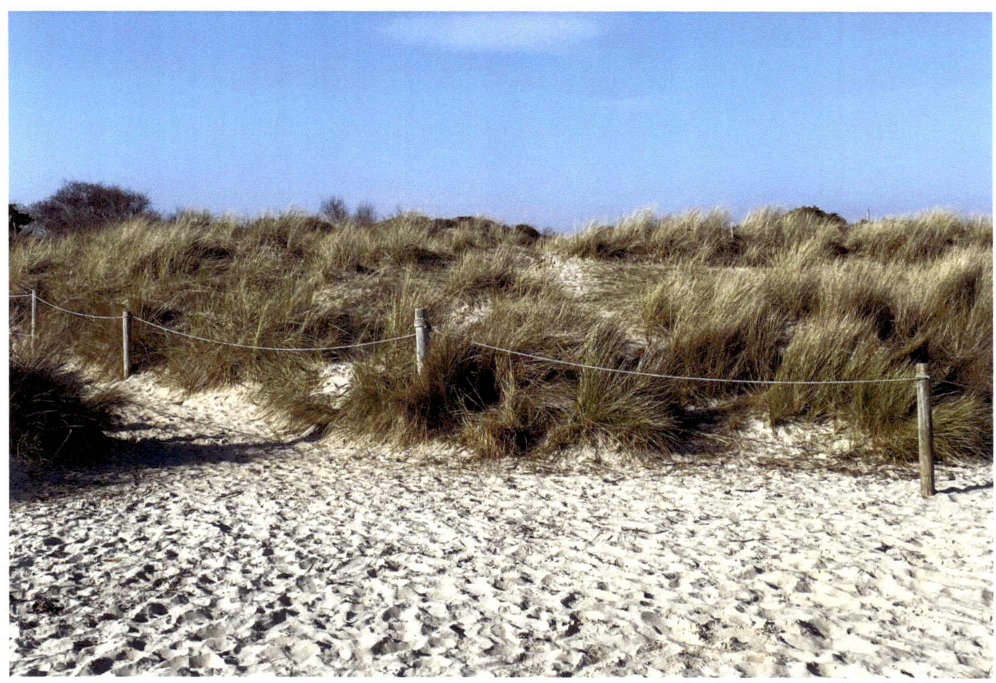

Sand dunes on the beach at Studland.

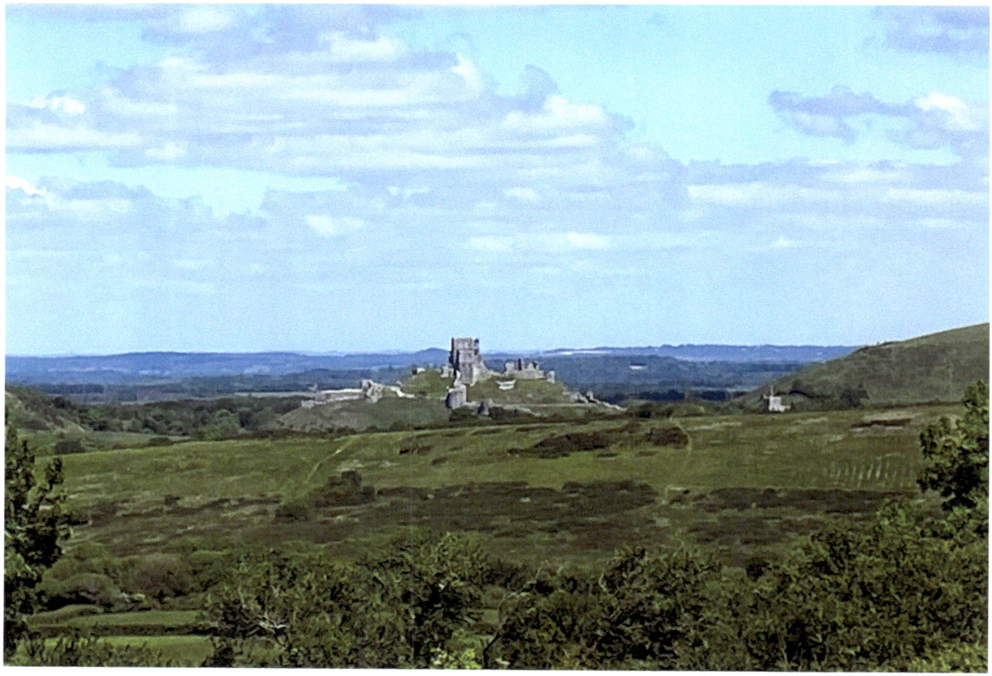

Corfe Common.

5. Treacherous Headlands and a Selection of Shipwrecks

The seas around Swanage have often witnessed vessels battling gale-force winds and tumultuous waves as they round the treacherous rocks and headlands.

During the eighteenth and nineteenth centuries, the rocky coastline was a recipe for shipping disasters, as it was not marked by lighthouses and this situation was compounded due to the lack of radar and modern navigational aids, which caused ships to hug the coast for ease of navigation and protection from the wind.

Another issue that reared its ugly head, from 1917 until the end of the First World War in 1918, was the intense German onslaught of submarine warfare, which resulted in increased shipping casualties including three off the coastline near Swanage.

Studland Bay and Handfast Point (Old Harry Rocks)

Old Harry is a chalk stack standing in the sea at Handfast Point on the Isle of Purbeck. It marks the Jurassic Coast's most easterly point and is believed to be named after Harry Paye, who was Poole's most notorious pirate. The Old Harry Rocks themselves are renowned for being dangerous, but the situation is made more treacherous as the area is subject to stormy weather and prevailing south-westerly winds.

Another factor in the locality is the deep-water Swash Channel, which extends from Studland Bay to the entrance of Poole Harbour, which, allied to the infamous Hook Sands on the adjacent Swash Bank, have frequently proved a disastrous combination for shipping over the years.

The entrance to Poole Harbour is also particularly dangerous, as its narrowness and strong tidal streams, especially at Spring Ebb tides, make it obligatory for a pilot provided by Poole Harbour Commission (PHC) to pilot vessels that are over 164 feet in length into the harbour.

Mortar Wreck – Thirteenth Century

The *Mortar Wreck* was discovered in 2020 by Trevor Small of Rocket Charters, Poole, and is so called due to the discovery on board of numerous Purbeck stone mortar bowls used for grinding grain into flour. It is the only known wreck in English waters from the period between the eleventh and fourteenth centuries. There are older wrecks, some dating to the Bronze Age, but these don't have any hull structure remaining. The *Mortar Wreck* is believed to have sunk during the reign of Henry III (r. 1216-1272), and was also carrying elaborately carved gravestones made from Purbeck stone; as well as cauldrons and other assorted medieval kitchen ware.

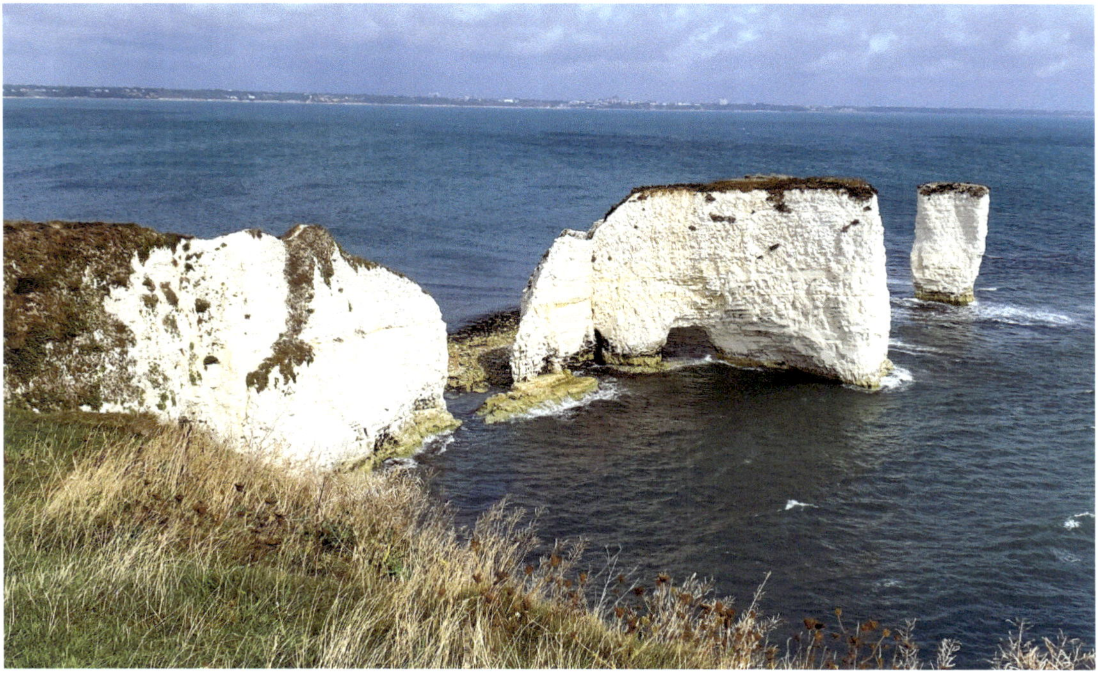

Old Harry.

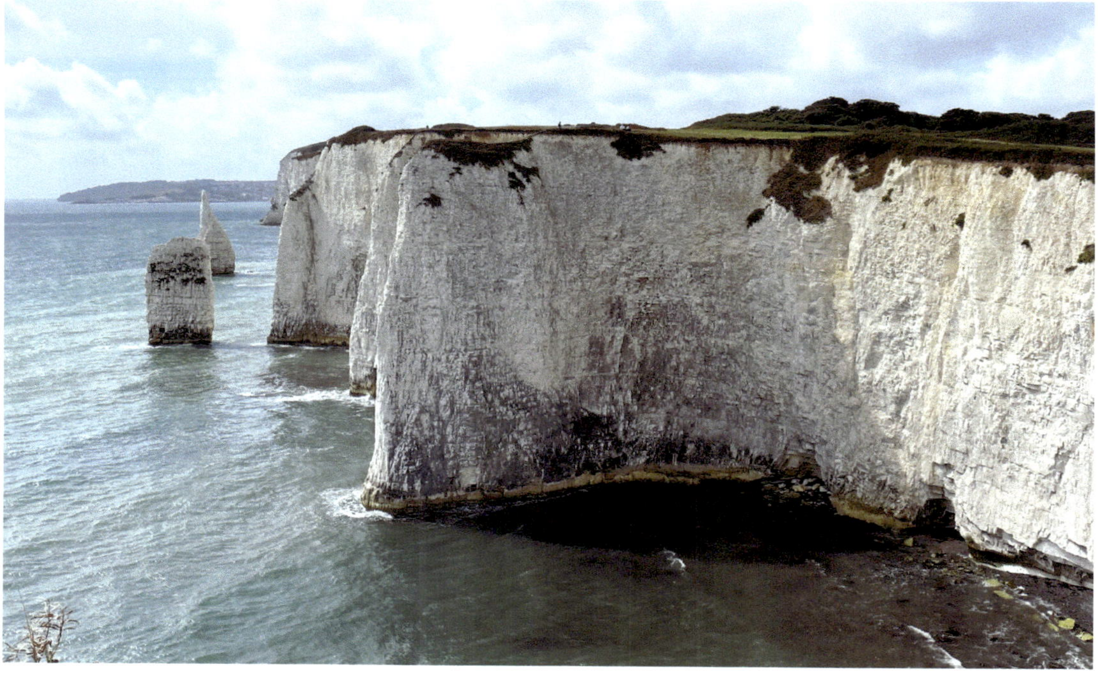

The Pinnacles – part of Old Harry Rocks.

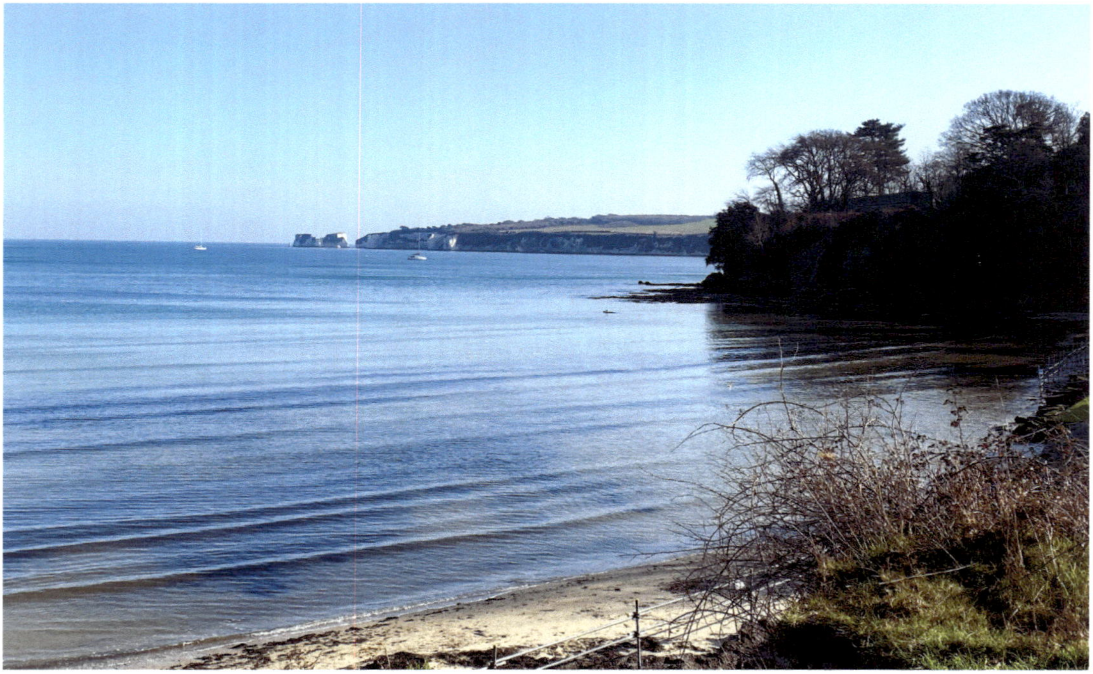

Studland Bay looking towards Old Harry.

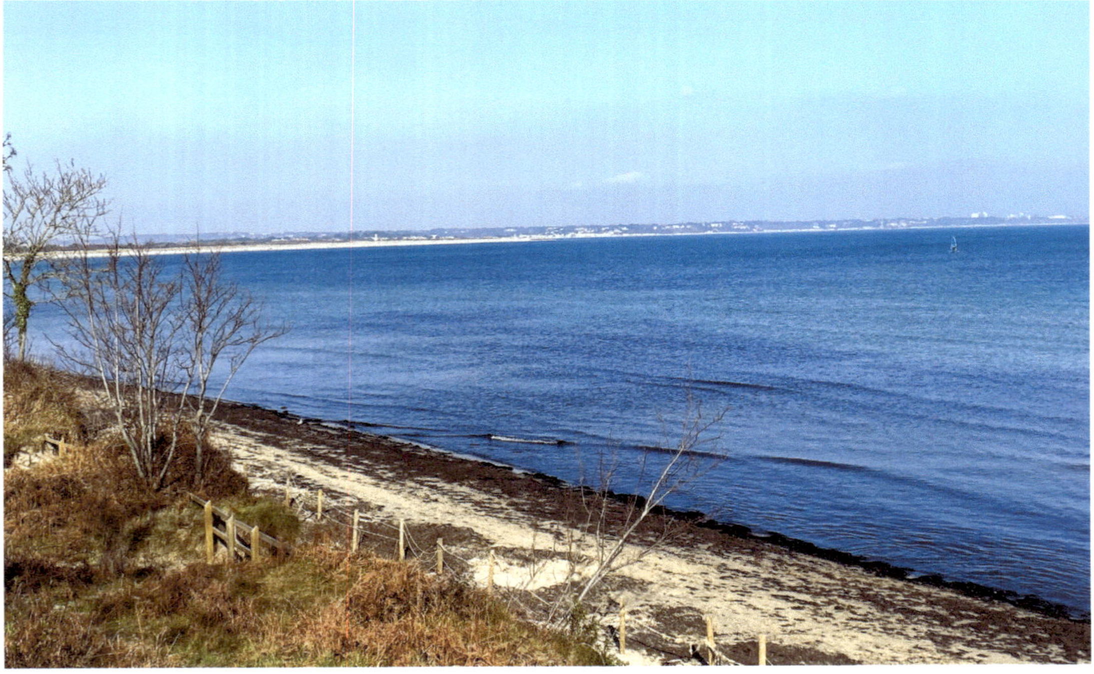

Studland Bay looking towards Poole Harbour.

San Salvador – 21 July 1588

Marine archaeologists have painstakingly pieced together the last throes of the *San Salvador*, a Spanish galleon which sank in Studland Bay on 21 July 1588 and was discovered in 1983 by divers from Hamworthy Sub Aqua Club.

It seems that the ship was blown up and captured during the Spanish Armada as she crossed Lyme Bay. It was then towed to Weymouth by a British crew in order to drop off the Spanish sailors for imprisonment and also to undergo repairs. The vessel was known to have been carrying the Spanish Paymaster General and a chest from the ship that contained gold can be seen in Weymouth museum. It then made its way to Portsmouth with a new British crew but foundered on the Old Harry Rocks en route.

Fame – March 1631

Another wreck discovered in the Swash Channel in the 1990s was the remains of a seventeenth-century, high-status, Dutch merchant ship, called *Fame,* which is believed to have come to grief whilst bound for the tropics. It is thought that the ship took refuge from a storm in Studland Bay, from where the anchor dragged resulting in the vessel becoming shipwrecked.

The site was designated as a protected historic wreck in 2004, and is now administered by Historic England.

In 2006, Bournemouth University students become involved in what is the largest underwater excavation since the *Mary Rose,* and have brought up over 1,000 artifacts, which are now in Poole Museum, including pottery, barrels, personal items, an iron cannon, and a 28-foot rudder with a face carved onto it.

Constitution – 17 January 1789

The *Constitution* was an American frigate that was returning to America from France with a consignment of exhibits intended for an exhibition about Paris that was taking place in the United States. The prevailing weather conditions and seas, as is common around this headland, were difficult and the vessel was driven onto the shingle that surrounds Old Harry Rocks. The crew removed as many heavy fittings as possible from the ship, before a government tug from Southampton and five other steamers managed to pull it clear. It then made its way to Portsmouth for repairs, but fortunately no significant damage was done.

Annie Margaretta – 24 January 1789

The following week, Old Harry did claim a ship: a 500-ton Norwegian schooner that was also on its way from France to America. It landed in more or less the same spot that the *Constitution* had. However, on this occasion the *Annie Margaretta* was not so fortunate, as it was totally destroyed by an easterly gale before assistance could arrive.

Peveril Point

PeverIl Ledge at Peveril Point consists of a sinister, shallow, serrated rocky reef of submerged and semi-submerged rocks, which stretch out into the bay and create a dangerous area of rough water on the race of the ebb tide. The area is marked by a red buoy and the combination of these factors has resulted in this headland being renowned as a veritable graveyard for shipping.

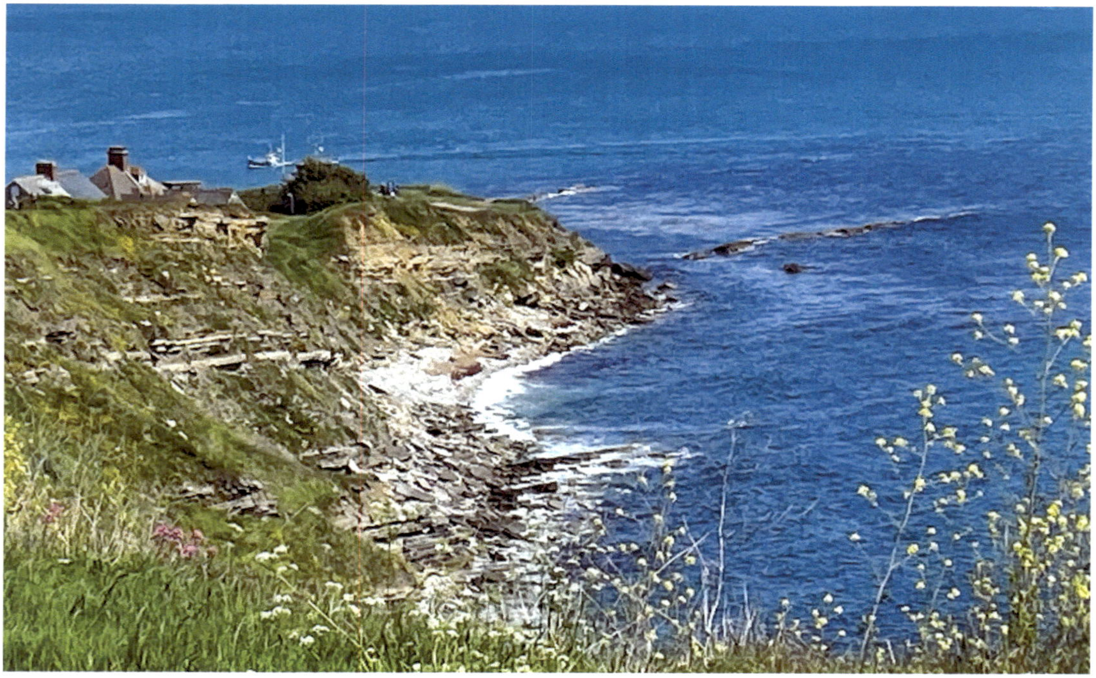

Peveril Point.

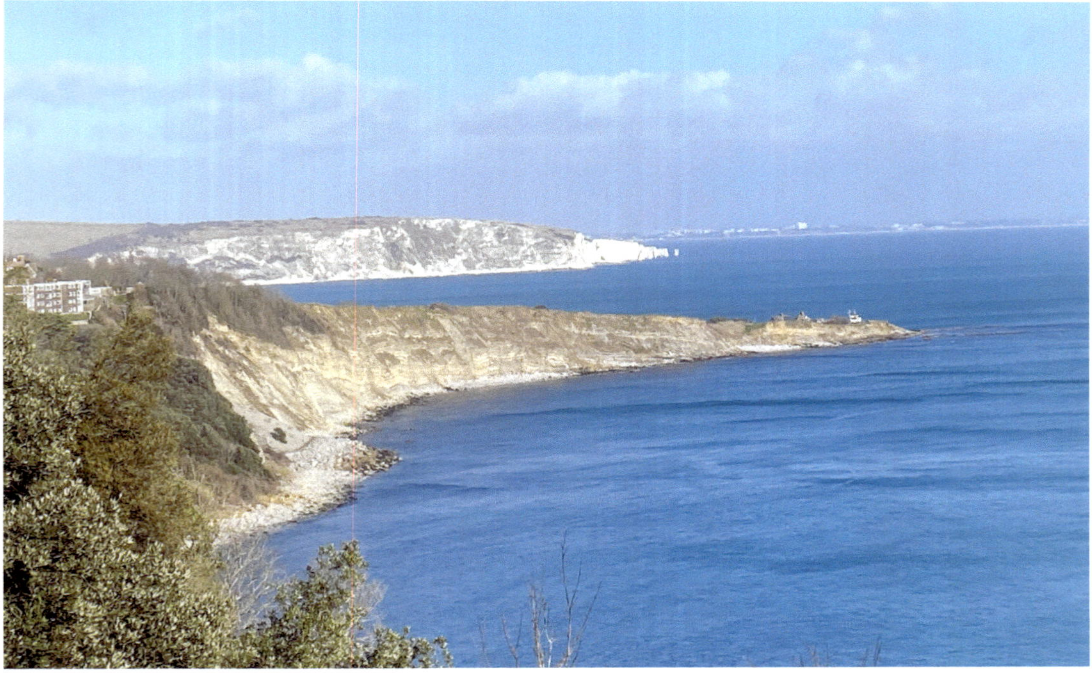

Peveril Point with Old Harry in the background.

Wild Wave – 23 January 1875

The brigantine *Wild Wave* of Exeter perished on the rocky reef at Peveril Ledge. The fierce mountainous waves caused the vessel to be dragged onto her beam and at 5.00 a.m. distress rockets were fired as the crew were ordered by Captain Bartlett to climb the rigging and hang on as best they could until they were hopefully seen by the citizens of Swanage in the morning light.

However, the crew had already been spotted and the coastguard boats were on their way. An eyewitness account from Mr C. J. Robinson, who recounted the story in the *Times*, tells of 'five sodden bundles, rather than living creatures, clustered together in a mass of tangled rigging'. He also describes the attempts to get a line on board and the rescue of four men and a boy in four oared open boats. Poole's lifeboat was launched, but after struggling through the horrendous gale, it only made it to the scene just as the last of the survivors had been rescued by the coastguard.

The grim story had a happy ending, but another happy outcome was that the Swanage Chief Coastguard Officer, Mr Lose, was awarded the RNLI silver medal for the coastguard rescue. Also Mr C. Robinson of Newton Manor House, Swanage, who related the story in the *Times*, pledged to establish a lifeboat at Swanage and with the help of George Burt, who matched his funding, he made good on his promise.

The Netto – 15 February 1900

The Norwegian brigantine *Netto* of Stavanger had deposited a cargo of coal at Plymouth and was bound for Poole with a cargo of salt when she was wrecked at Peveril Point.

The Swanage lifeboat *William Erle* was launched but was unable to get alongside the ship in the tumultuous seas. However, two coastguards managed to bravely clamber onto the wet rocks and were able to get a line on board using rocket apparatus and rescue the entire ship's complement, shortly before the vessel split in two.

Summer Song – 9 October 2010

The 36-foot yacht *Summer Song* ran aground at Peveril Ledge in a fierce gale in the early hours of the morning. A crew member made a mayday call to Portland Coastguard at 5.20 a.m., who in turn alerted Swanage Lifeboat Station, who affected a rescue.
Portland coastguard watch manager Dominic Lonsdale said of the incident:

> Within 40 minutes of the initial mayday call the casualties were safely ashore with an ambulance en route. This illustrates the speed at which rescue resources are able to be dispatched to those in need and with strong easterly winds and the yacht being pounded on to rocks this was certainly an urgent call for help.

Anvil Point and Anvil Point Lighthouse

The treacherous seas and dangerous rocks around Anvil Point, which lies within the grounds of Durlston Country Park, led to demands for the construction of a lighthouse. It was built from locally quarried stone and completed in 1881. It was opened by Joseph Chamberlain, the Minister of Transport, who was the father of Neville Chamberlain, the former Prime Minister.

The beam was originally provided by a paraffin vapour burner, before being converted to run on mains electricity in 1960.

In 1991, the lighthouse became fully automated with a beam that produces a white flash every ten seconds and extends as far west as Portland Bill and as far east as Christchurch. It is controlled from the Trinity House Operations Control Centre in Harwich and is currently utilised as two holiday cottages.

Alexandrovna – 29 April 1882

The Scottish-built 1,250-ton Liverpool sailing ship *Alexandrovna* was being blown in atrocious weather conditions onto the ragged rocks just west of Anvil Point.

Some people on the cliffs near Tilly Whim Quarry saw that the ship was in obvious danger and one of the group ran the 2 miles to Swanage to alert the coastguard.

Meanwhile the coastguards at St Alban's Station had also become aware of the situation and were hurrying to the scene with life-saving equipment. However, such was the ferocity of the storm that in the ten minutes it took rescuers to reach the stricken ship, it had become little more than driftwood.

The entire ship's complement of seventy-seven were drowned and the ship was only identified because one of the bodies was found attached to a lifebuoy bearing the ship's name.

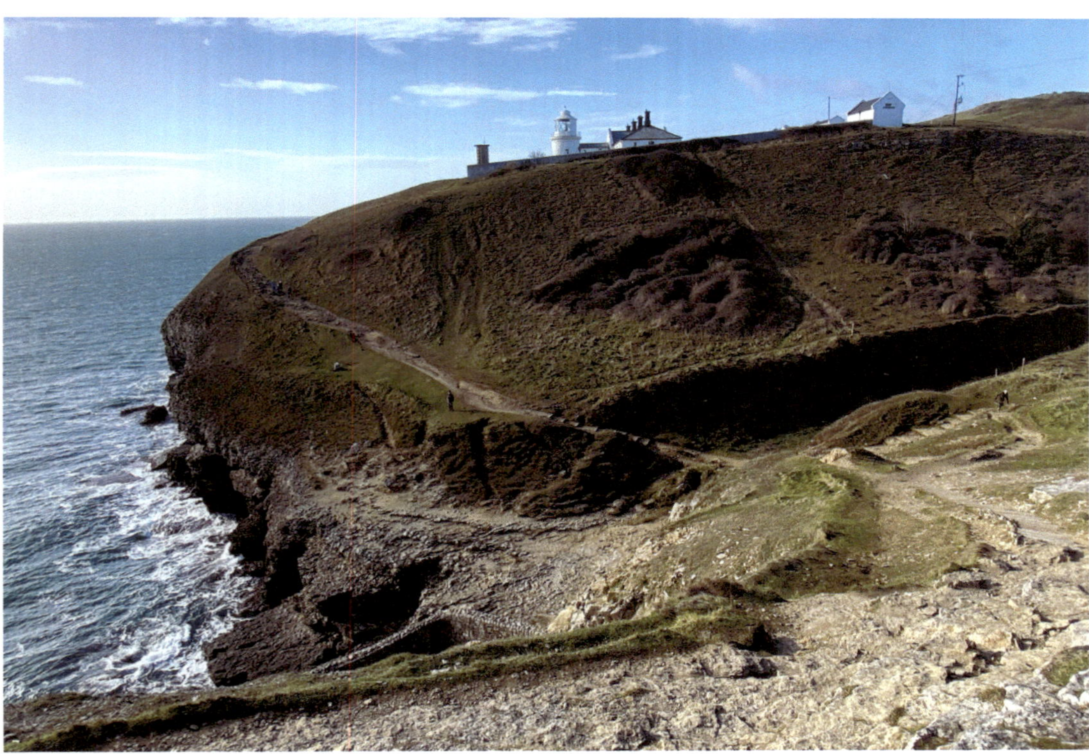

Anvil Point.

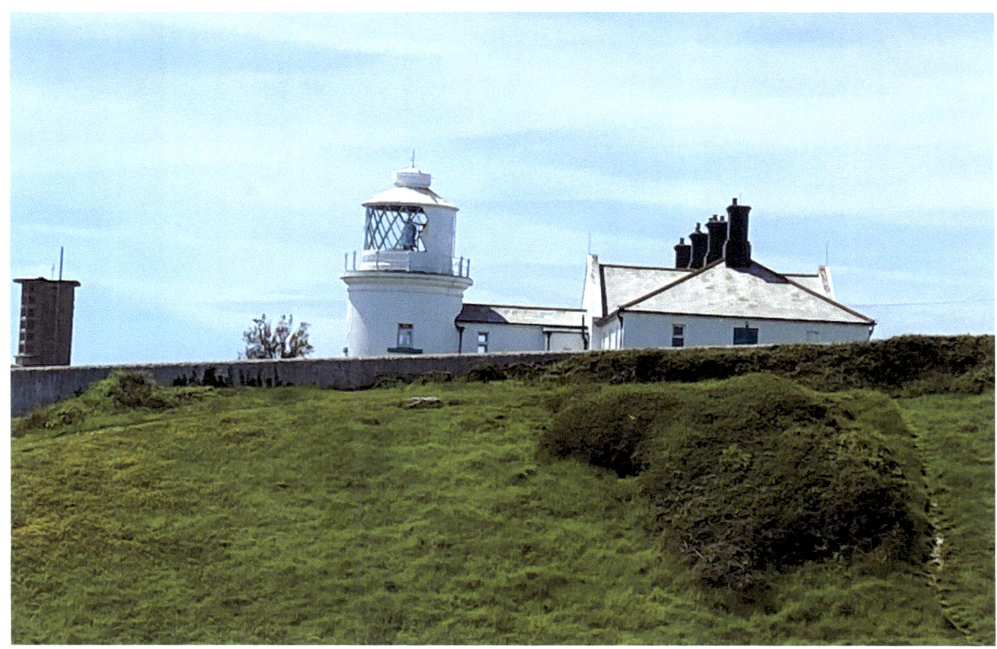

Anvil Point Lighthouse.

Plantin – 26 April 1917

The *Plantin* was an 84-ton steam vessel requisitioned by the Admiralty for use as a minesweeper. Unfortunately, it fell afoul of a mine itself, 3 miles east of Anvil Point, and sank, with only one member of the crew of ten surviving.

Kyarra – 24 May 1918

The *Kyarra* was a former Australian luxury liner requisitioned for military service, initially as a hospital ship and then as a troop carrier. It was making her way from Tilbury to Devonport in order to collect some cargo, and wounded Australian servicemen, who were to be transported to Sydney, when she was struck by a torpedo fired from a German U-boat.

As the ship sank, the lifeboats on board were deployed saving the 140 passengers. However, five crew members lost their lives in the initial explosion and one died later due to the severity of his injuries.

The wreck site is now renowned as Dorset's most popular dive spot.

DID YOU KNOW?
Marmite jars consisting of ceramic pots with lead lids were found at the wreck. If only that shipment had made it through to Australia, then the Australians may have been saved from having to eat Vegemite.

Aparima – November 1917

The *Aparima* had previously been a cargo liner based in New Zealand, before being requisitioned as a defensively armed British merchant ship. The vessel was making her way from London to Barry, with Captain Stokely-Doorly hugging the coastline in an attempt to avoid U-boats. However, his efforts proved to be in vain and he was torpedoed as he rounded Anvil Point. The ship sunk almost immediately and fifty-six of the 110 crew were lost.

St Alban's Head

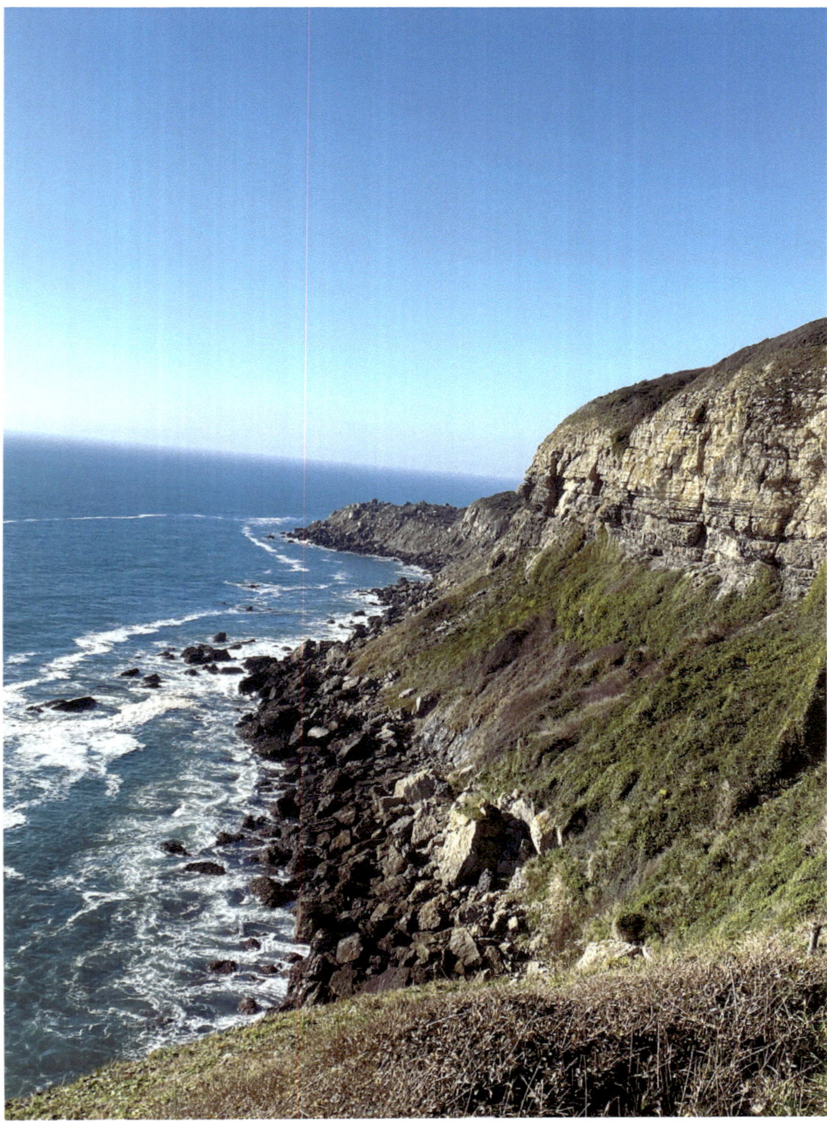

St Alban's Head.

St Alban's Ledge

St Alban's Ledge extends 2.5 miles south-west of the headland and forms a treacherous race, which can be seen as a churning mass of white water, even on a cloudy day. In addition to this the strong currents and dangerous tides have meant that over the years only Chessil Beach in the region has seen more fatalities.

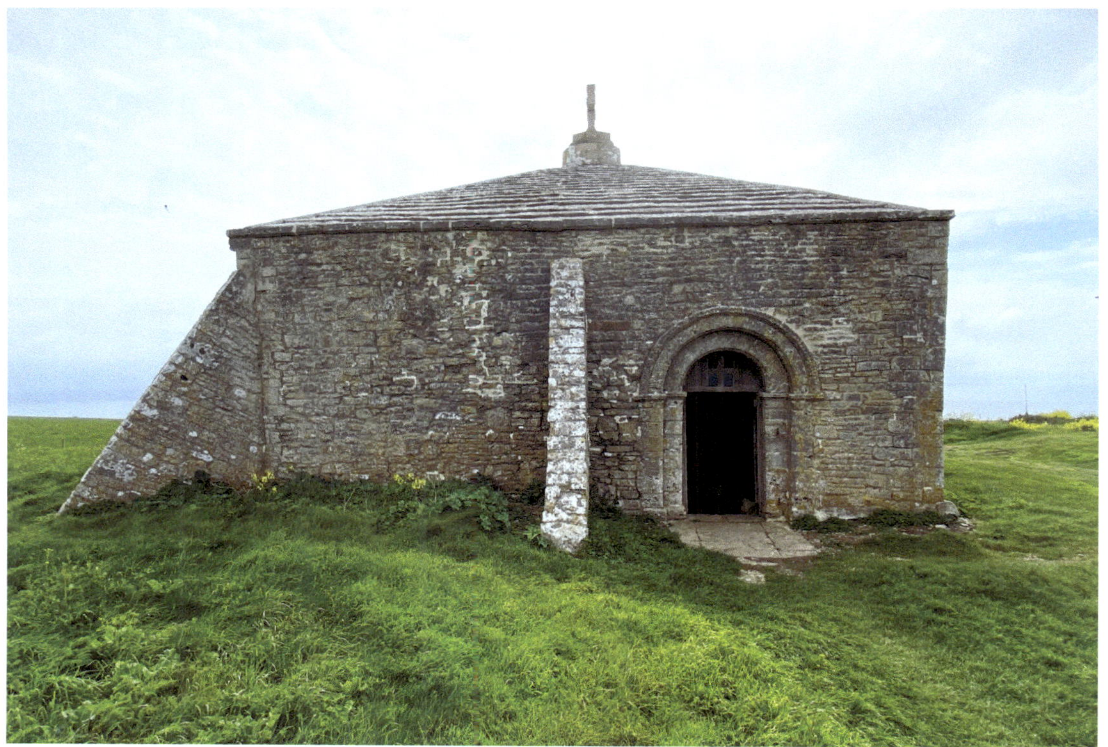

St Aldhelm's Chapel was built in the thirteenth century and is named after the first Bishop of Sherborne.

Pillar of Rock

At St Alban's Head, there is a pillar of rock that was created by quarrymen. It provides a marker for seafarers and in particular, skippers of small boats who prefer to cut in close to the headland in order to avoid going through or around the area of rough sea and savage currents of the St Alban's Race.

Halsewell – 1 January 1786

On New Year's Day 1786, the 758-ton, East Indiaman the *Halsewell* set sail on an ill-fated journey from Gravesend to Madras, India. It was commanded by Captain Richard Pierce, who was considered to be one of the company's most senior men and was due to retire after completing this voyage. The total ship's complement of 240 passengers and crew included troops being sent to various garrisons in India, as well as the captain's two daughters and two of his nieces.

The ship had not gone very far when the journey took a disastrous turn for the worse as the top sails and main sail were severely damaged in a blizzard in the Dover Straits, leaving the ship floundering and being driven onto the cliffs of the Kent coast.

Masts and sails were cut down and further desperate attempts were made to turn the vessel from the wind, resulting in the coxswain and four others being thrown overboard

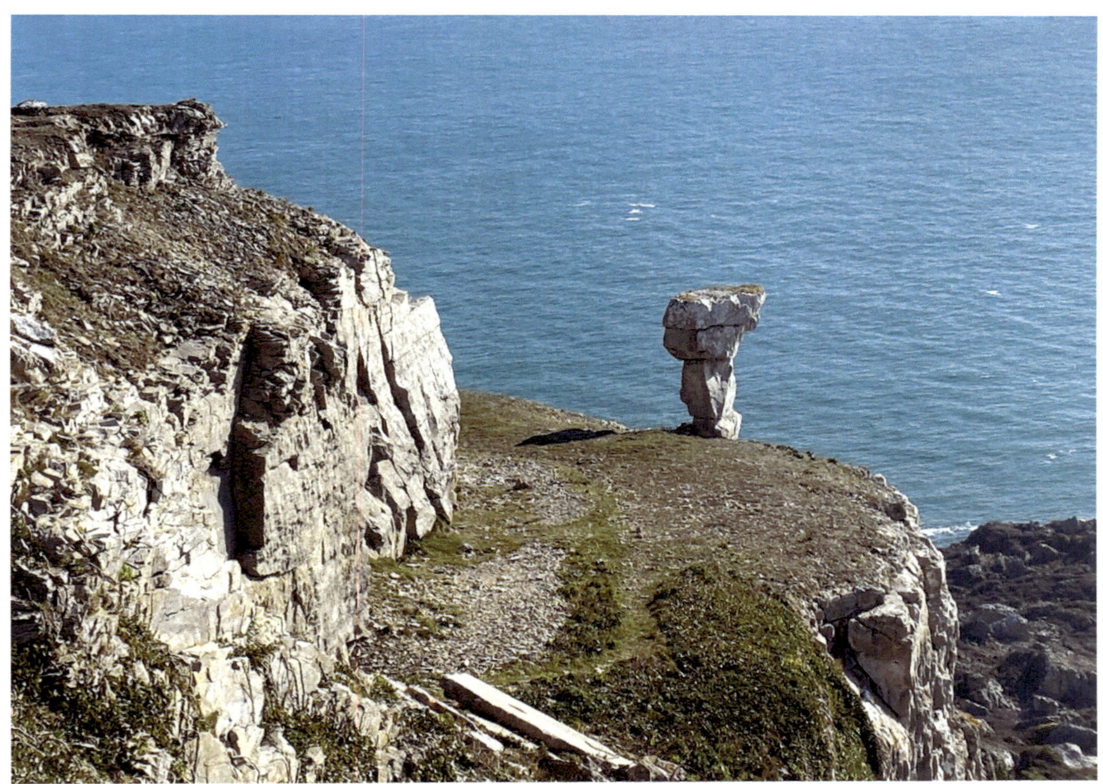

The Pillar of Rock at St Alban's Head.

and drowning. The weather conditions deteriorated further and so did conditions on board, as the hull had become damaged and had started taking on water, causing the ship to roll dangerously in the rough seas.

It was now evident that to get to India would be impossible and the decision was taken to head to Portsmouth for repairs instead. Accordingly, the ship limped on its way, making painfully slow progress, as it took over twelve hours to make it to Portland Bill and successfully round the headland, with the intention of taking shelter in Studland Bay for the night. However, at 11.00 p.m. the ferocious storm abated to a degree, allowing the crew to see what lay ahead of them and unfortunately it became apparent that they had been driven from their intended course and were now perilously close to St Alban's Head. Accordingly, a distress cannon was fired to alert any potential rescuers on the shore.

Captain Pierce ordered the crew to drop anchor in order to ride out the storm and to prevent the ship being pushed closer to the headland. However, the heavy swell and the tides caused the anchors to drag and in the early hours of the morning, the *Halsewell* struck the jagged rocky reef on the approach to Seacombe Cliffs, near Winspit, a mile away from St Alban's Head.

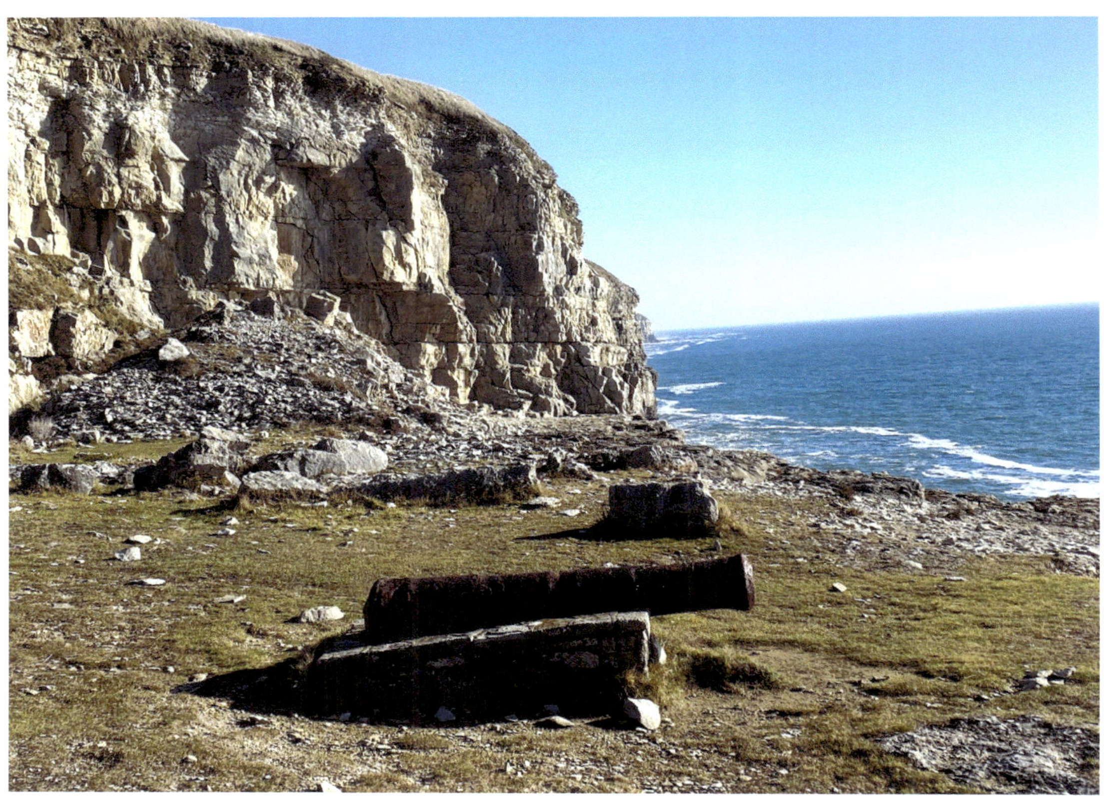

At Hedbury Quarry, there is a large cannon mounted on a plinth, which is thought to have been recovered from the shipwreck of the *Halsewell* and placed there in recognition of the victims of the disaster.

A seaman named Henry Moreton attempted to get ashore by negotiating a spar from the side of the ship that had come to rest on the cliffs. A wave knocked him off, but fortuitously carried him to relative safety onto a shelf at the rear of a cave within the cliff face. Twenty-seven others also managed to escape the ship and took some sort of refuge in the cavern within the cliff, now known as the 'Halsewell Rock', although the cavern has long since collapsed. From there they struggled to join Moreton on his safer upper shelf, but several perished in the attempt.

However, two agile crew members somehow managed to scale the hazardous cliffs and make it to the nearest habitation of Easington Farm to raise the alarm. The farmer in turn alerted the local quarrymen in the village of Worth Matravers and they swiftly made their way to the scene to offer assistance. They worked tirelessly throughout the day and eighty-eight people were saved, although fourteen died in the dangerous extraction from the ship and cliffs. In total 166 people died including Captain Pierce and his daughters and nieces.

The *Halsewell* disaster is regarded as one of the worst shipwrecks of all time and formed the basis of a Charles Dickens novel, *The Long Journey*.

The Legend of St Aldhelm's Chapel

St Aldhelm's Chapel dates back to the thirteenth century and is one the oldest churches in England. However, it is considered that it was in use long before that time as a Christian hermitage.

It is also believed by some that its original use may have been as a watchtower guarding the sea from the south for Corfe Castle. Its square shape and corners, which correspond to the four cardinal compass points, allied to the fact that it only has one window looking out to sea add credence to this theory, as does the fact that its location is some way from the village of Worth Matravers.

Another possibility is that it served as a marker for mariners, while others believe that it may have been built by a father grieving for his daughter, who, along with her husband she had recently married, were lost at sea.

HMT *Arfon*, 30 April 1917

HMT *Arfon* was a trawler requisitioned by the Royal Navy, which operated from Portland Harbour Naval Base and was engaged in sweeping mines from the shipping lanes of Dorset.

After three years of successful mine sweeping the vessel's number was finally up when it was struck by a mine itself 35 miles south of St Alban's Head. The resulting explosion caused the loss of ten of its crew including its captain, John Abrams. Three crew members survived having been blown overboard by the explosion.

The *Arfon* was struck by a mine laid by *UC61*, a U-boat that was also responsible for sinking eleven Allied vessels in total before it was finally sunk itself in July 1917.

SS *L'Atlantique* – 5 January 1933

The SS *L'Atlantique* was a French owned luxury liner that plied its trade between France and South America.

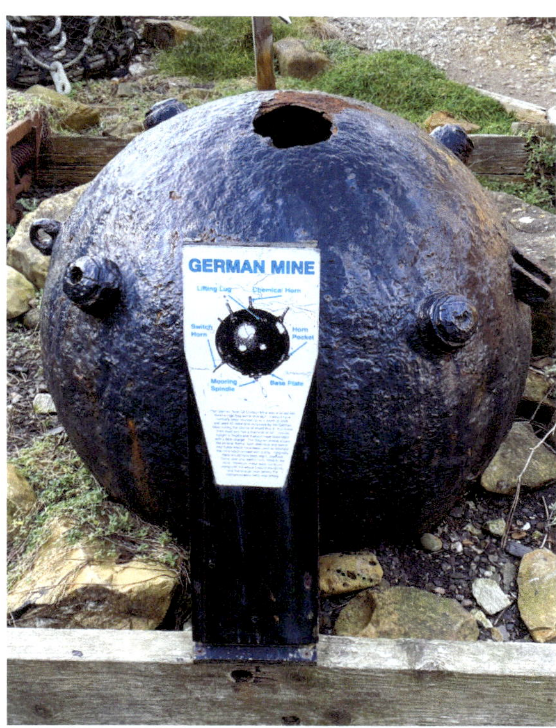

This German Type GZ Contact Mine from the Second World War was found in Kimmeridge Bay.

Only the crew were aboard on that fateful day as it travelled between Bordeaux and Le Havre, France, in order to undergo a refit. It was in the English Channel about 25 miles off the coast of Guernsey when it caught fire, and by late afternoon of that day it had drifted towards St Alban's Head. The fire escalated rapidly and by dawn the following day the crew were ordered to abandon ship by their captain.

Consequently, the crew were in the water in their ship's lifeboats when the Dutch steamship *Achilles,* responding to the distress signal, arrived on the scene and managed to pick up the majority of the crew. Another ship in attendance was the SS *Ford Castle*, a collier ship. The first mate Thomas Henry Wilmott of Sunderland was the coxswain of a lifeboat from that ship, which went alongside the burning liner and managed to rescue twenty people, who were still on board. Wilmott was later rewarded for his bravery when he was presented with the Medaille de Sauvetage.

The liner was then towed, still burning, to Cherbourg by nine tugs, several of whom also sustained fire damage as a result.

Aeolian Sky – 3 November 1979

The 14,000-ton Greek freighter *Aeolian Sky* was built in 1978 at the Japanese Hashihama shipyard. It was rounding Anvil Point en route to Dar es Salaam, Tanzania, when it was in a collision with a much smaller 2,400-ton German ship, MV *Anna Knueppel.* Strangely the smaller ship emerged virtually unscathed, whereas the larger vessel was holed near the bows, leaving the crew no option but to abandon ship. A call went out to the Royal Navy

Air Station at Lee-on-Solent and the sixteen crew members were successfully airlifted onto a Dutch Navy destroyer.

The stricken *Aeolian Sky* was then towed by tug towards Southampton. However, due to the toxic cargo of all manner of poisonous chemicals including paint thinners, liquid chlorine and aerosols, allied to the high possibility that the vessel could go down, it was thought prudent to alter the destination to the nearer port of Weymouth.

Unfortunately the next day brought gale-force winds and heavy seas, causing the *Aeolian Sky* to indeed sink 5 miles from St Alban's Head. A major alert was then initiated in an attempt to control the environmental catastrophe. In addition to the toxic cargo, barbed wire, two diesel locomotives and a fleet of Land Rovers also went down with the ship, as well as cases containing a consignment of 60,000 Seychelles rupees.

The police made enquiries regarding the missing rupees, resulting in various fishermen and divers being asked to hand back the few handfuls of missing notes that had been found.

Kimmeridge Ledges and Chapman's Pool
To the west of St Alban's Head is Chapman's Pool, a crescent-shaped cove which in some ways can be considered a poor man's Lulworth Cove, although it has the advantage that because of its inaccessibility, it is far less busy.

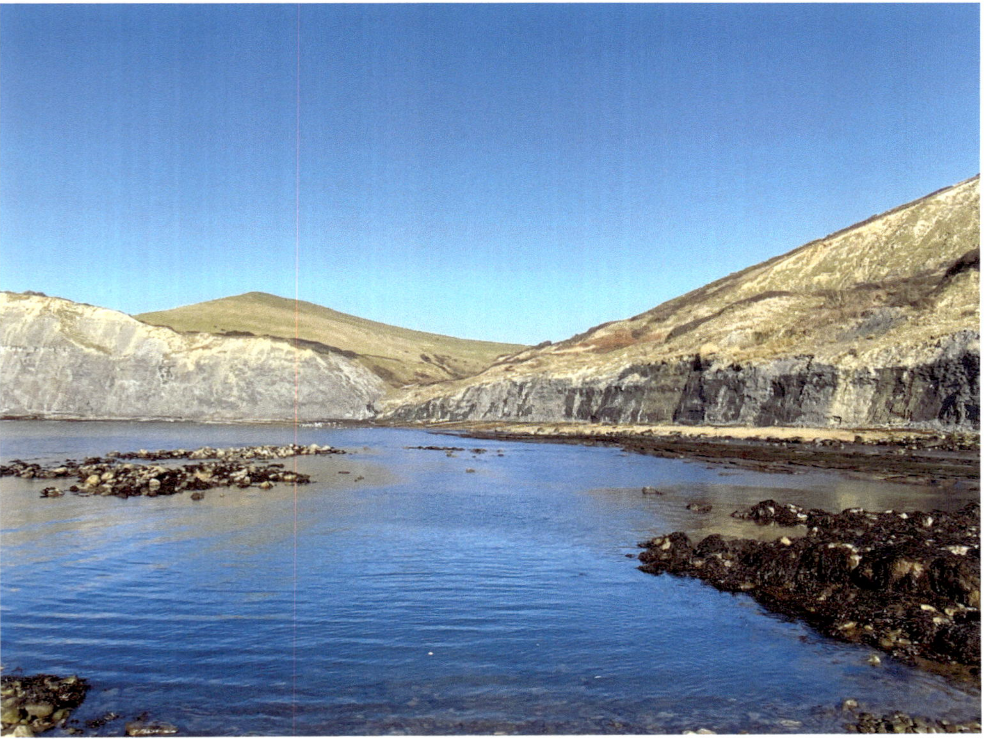

Chapman's Pool.

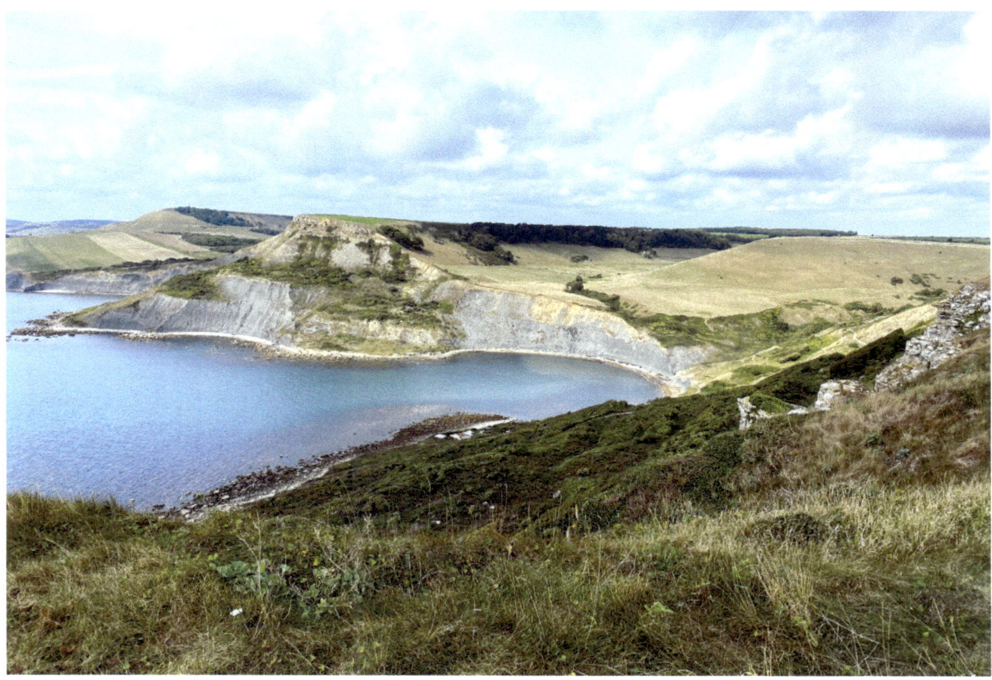

Chapman's Pool from above.

To the west of Chapman's Pool are the dangerous Kimmeridge Ledges, which consist of long flat layers of rock, extending up to half a mile off shore; then further west on the western aspect of Kimmeridge Bay is the hazardous Broad Bench, which generates waves up to 15 feet high.

HMS *Skylark* – 25 April 1845

HMS *Skylark* made its way to Portsmouth under the temporary command of the master, William Crane, as the ship's actual commander, Lieutenant Morris, was confined to his cabin due to a severe attack of gout. There was very little wind and all sails were set. However, on the morning of 25 April, the ship and crew of 110 found themselves enveloped by fog, as Crane continued on his merry way, without altering the configuration of the sails. Accordingly the vessel made excellent progress until it struck Coalpit Ledge, one of the Kimmeridge Ledges.

The coastguard managed to rescue the entire crew, but Crane was dismissed from the service at a subsequent court martial.

Georgiana – 11 July 1866

The 400-ton French barque *Georgiana*, carrying a cargo of coffee, cocoa and mahogany, was driven by a ferocious storm into Chapman's Pool, where the crew of thirteen and two passengers were rescued by coastguards, who fired a rocket line. The cargo was largely salvaged but the ship was totally destroyed.

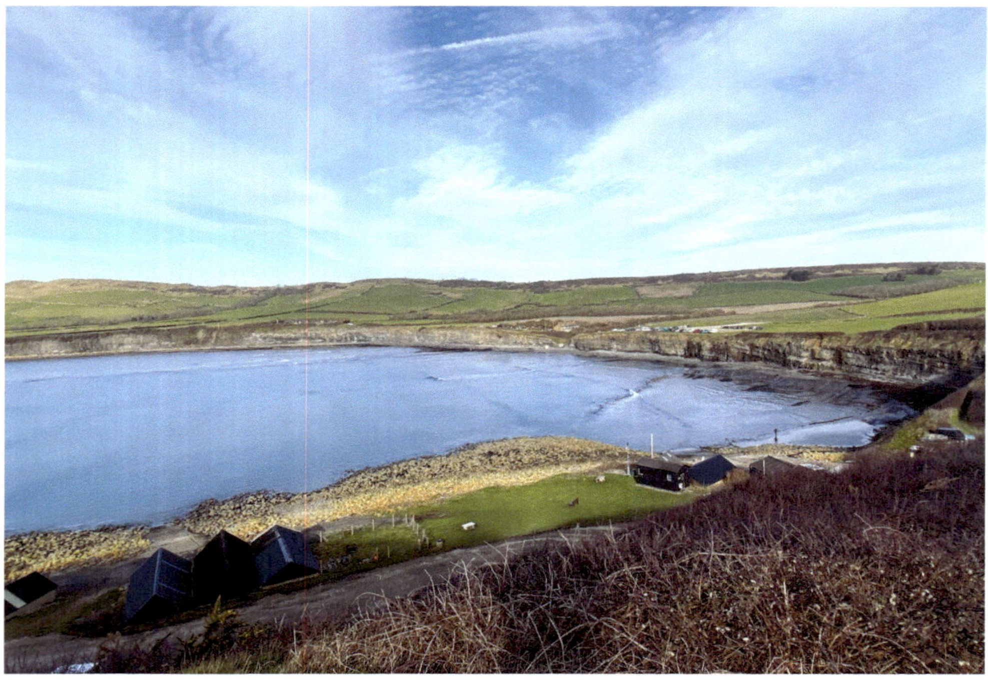

Kimmeridge Bay.

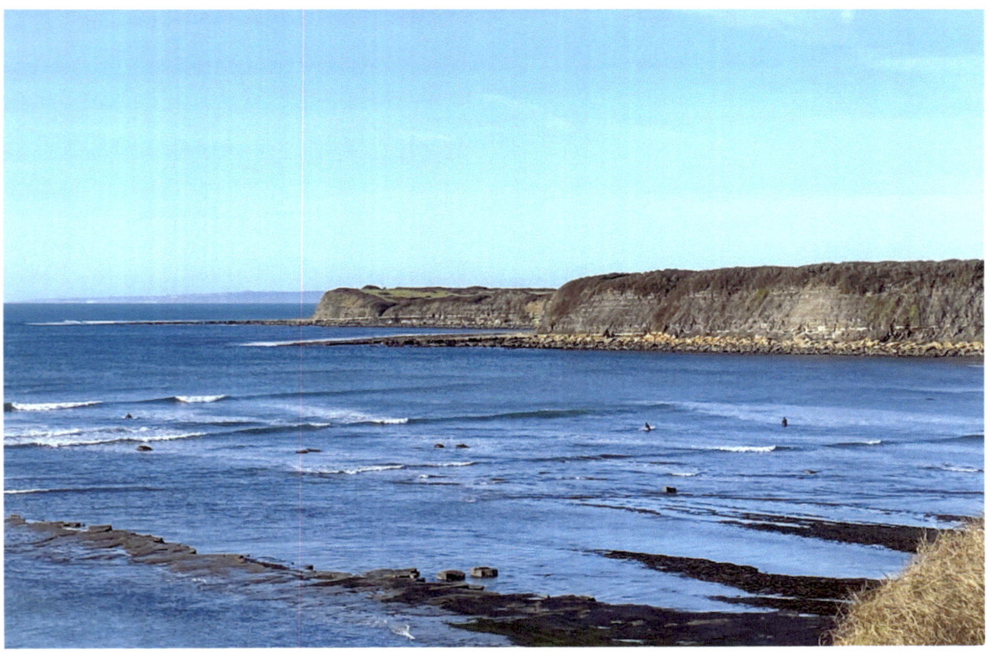

Surfers enjoying the ledge-enhanced waves to the east of Kimmeridge Bay. There are also ledges within the bay.

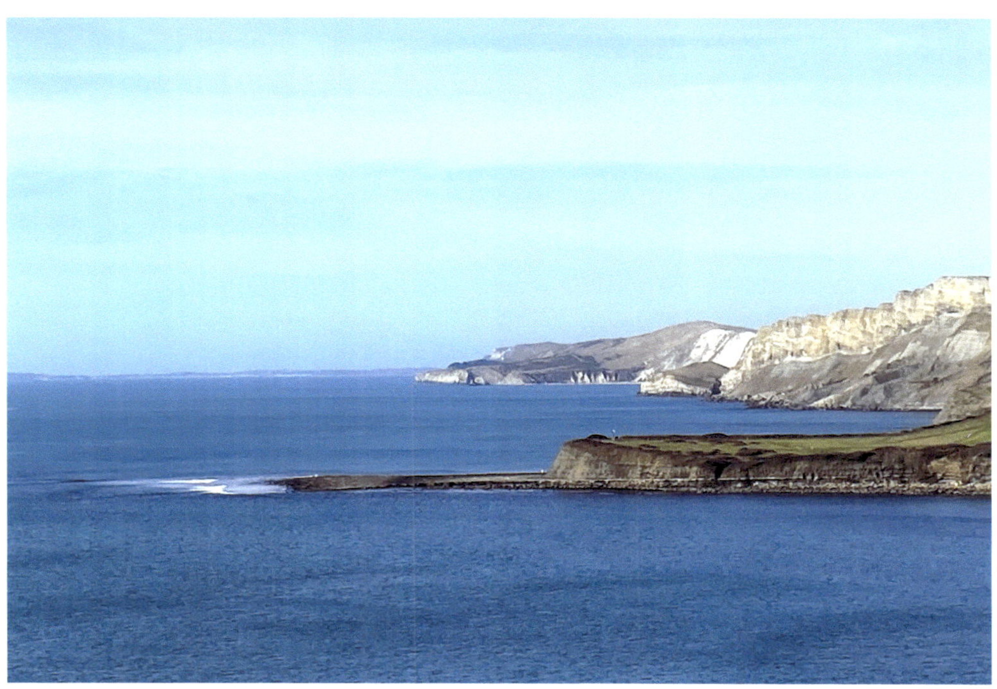

Broad Bench, Kimmeridge.

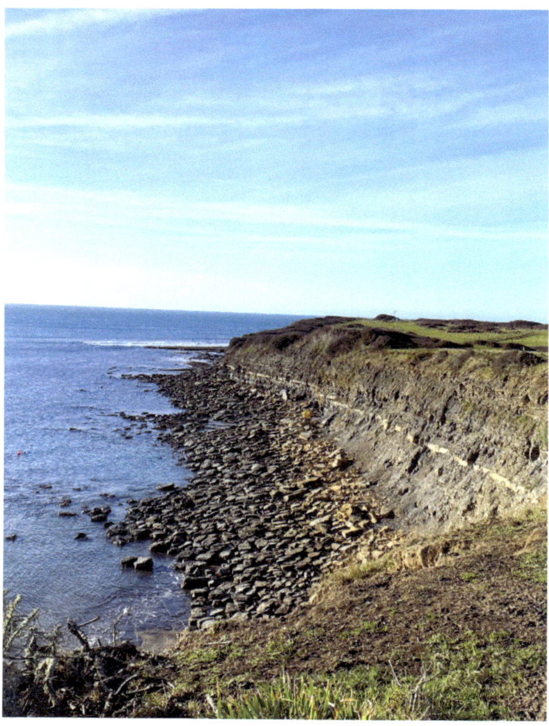

A close-up view of Broad Bench.

Lifeboat Station at Chapman's Pool

Shortly after the rescue of the *Georgiana* and due to the loss of many lives in the vicinity in the 1800s, a lifeboat station was built in 1867 at Chapman's Pool, after local pressure.

However, the station closed in 1880 due to the expense of maintaining the building, which was frequently damaged due to landslips. Another problem was that due to its remote location, volunteers were unable to get there quickly and when they did arrive, launching was difficult in stormy conditions.

The building can still be seen today and serves as a fishing hut.

Liberty – 1868

The decision to install a lifeboat station at Chapman's Pool was soon shown to be ill-conceived when, shortly afterwards, the schooner *Liberty* was damaged at Broad Bench, a quarter of a mile from the shore.

The Chapman's Pool lifeboat crew valiantly tried to launch their boat, *George Scott*, but despite numerous attempts were unable to do so into the teeth of the raging storm. Meanwhile the *Liberty* broke up and only the upper rigging protruded from the violent sea, as crew members grimly hung on for dear life.

A coastguard boat was launched but their boat wasn't large enough to cope with the fearsome gale and they were unable to get close enough to the ship. The rocket lines they fired all fell short, meaning they had no option but to watch in agony as the crew members, one by one, fell exhausted into a watery grave.

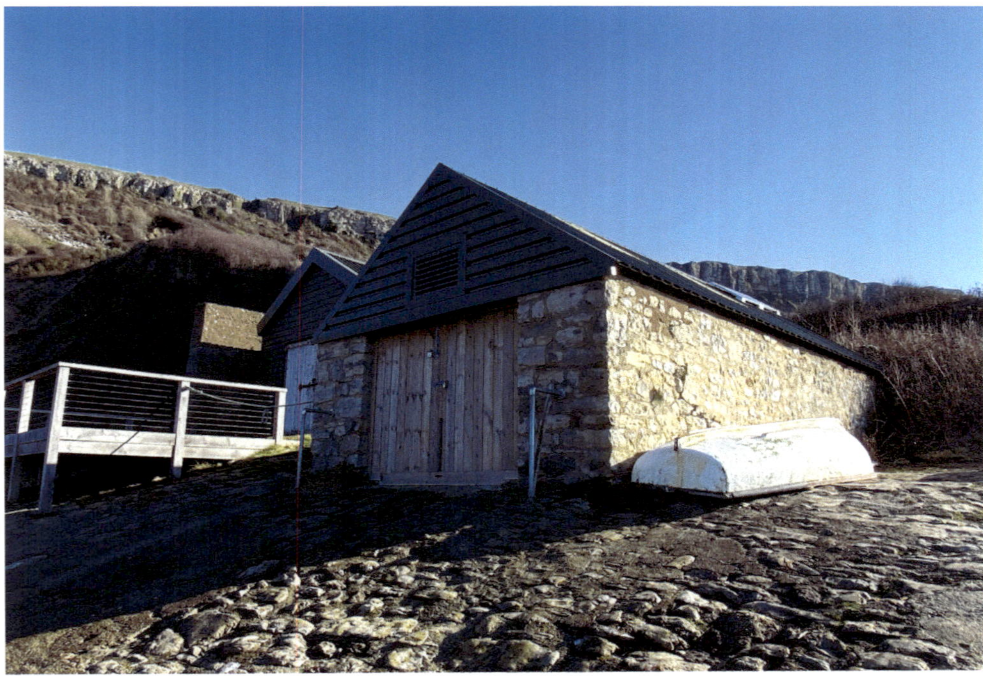

The old lifeboat station, Chapman's Pool.

After this debacle an alternative lifeboat station was established in 1868 at Kimmeridge, with a lifeboat named *Mary Heape*. It was located close to Broad Bench in order to be better positioned to get to ships in distress on the Kimmeridge Ledges.

Stralsund – 8 December 1872

The Kimmeridge station closed in 1880, as it's remote location caused the same issue that the Chapman's Pool lifeboat station had suffered from, in that it was unfeasible for the crew to get to quickly. Another factor was that Swanage also had a lifeboat station by then.

However, during the period of the lifeboat's existence, the Kimmeridge lifeboat crew did successfully rescue the *Stralsund*, a German ship which was blown onto the dangerous Kimmeridge Ledges.

SS *Treveal* – 9 January 1920

SS *Treveal*, a 3,226-ton freighter, was heading for Dundee on the return journey from Calcutta, India. This was the ship's maiden voyage and it carried a cargo of jute and manganese.

Unfortunately, the vessel floundered on the Kimmeridge Ledges and then as a result turned beam first into Chapman's Pool, where the fierce waves caused her to capsize.

A Portland dock tug attempted to assist the stricken ship, but was unable to make any progress in the appalling weather conditions. A further two tugs were then sent from Weymouth, one of which was towing a lifeboat. However, as the lifeboat attempted to

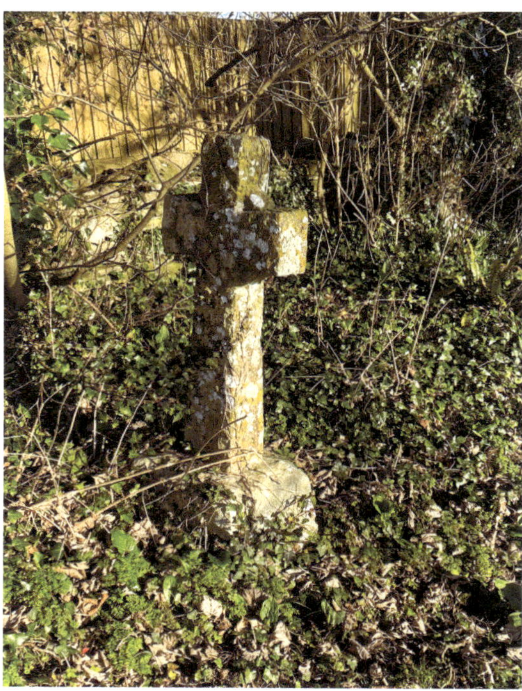

A grave in St Nicholas' churchyard, Worth Matravers, is the final resting place of two bodies of unknown sailors from the SS *Treveal*.

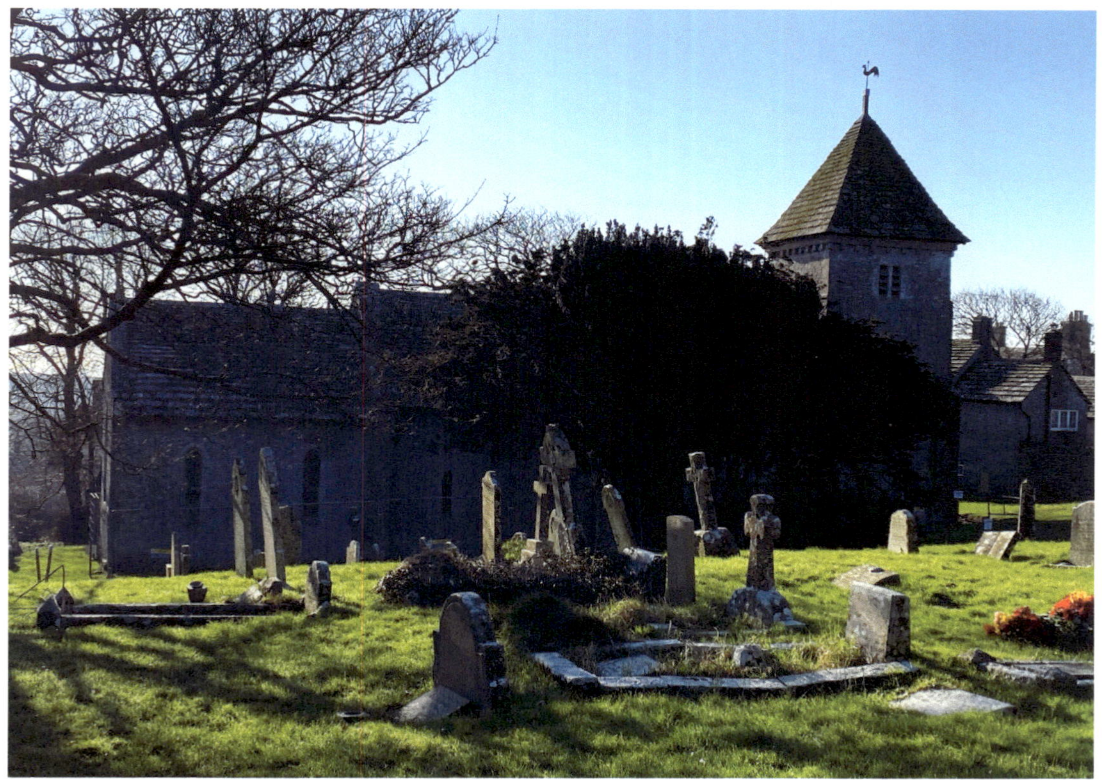

St Nicholas' Church, Worth Matravers.

get close to the ship, it too got into difficulty, but was then fortuitously swept into Poole Harbour and safety.

Meanwhile the crew of the SS *Treveal* were ordered to abandon ship by Captain Charles Paynter, as he had noticed that the ship was split along its side. Accordingly the crew left the ship in two boats and rowed towards the shore. However, both boats capsized and only seven of the forty-three crew members reached the shore to be rescued by the local vicar and a fisherman. Captain Paynter was among those who lost their lives.

An inquest into the SS *Treveal* tragedy was held in the village pub. The Square and Compass (see Smugglers) and later a week-long enquiry took place at Stanley Hall in Weymouth.

DID YOU KNOW?
St Nicholas is a popular church name in this part of Dorset. St Nicholas is the patron saint of sailors and thieves, so maybe the maritime and smuggling history explains it. Of course he is also the patron saint of children, as in Santa Claus.

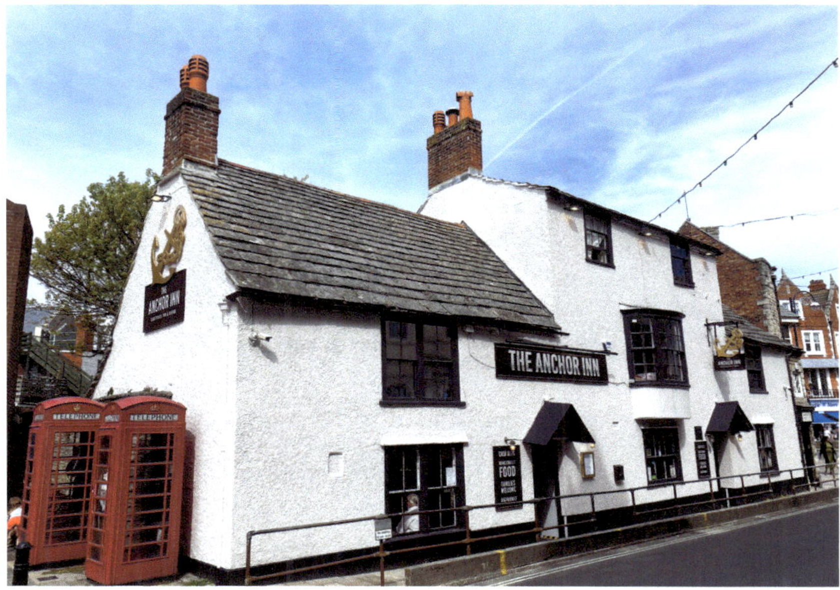

The survivors of the SS *Treveal* were put up in the Anchor Inn, Swanage, a pub with an interesting heritage having also been a Royal Mail coaching inn where coaches left for Wareham, as well as a market house on market days. It was even a place where local men barricaded themselves in to avoid the press gangs when they sought mariners for Royal Naval ships at Poole Quay.

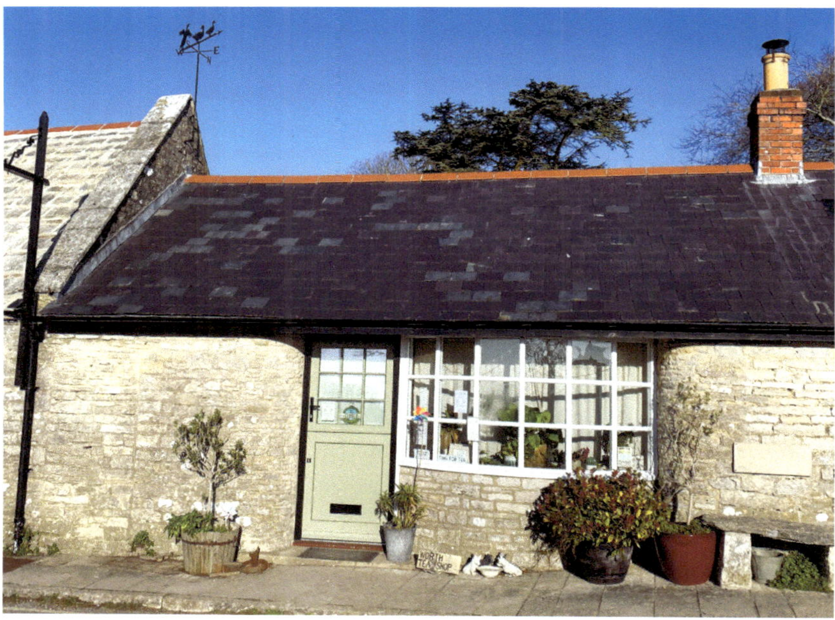

The dead bodies reclaimed from the sea after the SS *Treveal* disaster were transported in carts to Worth Matravers and laid out in the Reading Room (now Worth Matravers Tea Room). The bodies were then transported to St Ives, Cornwall, where the crew hailed from.

National Coastwatch Institution (NCI)
In the early days, the main concern of coastguards was to prevent smuggling. However, after the demise of smuggling they focused more on their alternative role of spotting ships in distress and rescuing mariners, a function which they undertook admirably until 1990, when the government closed numerous stations with the intention of relying more on electronic surveillance.

This inevitably proved to be a short-sighted move and after a tragedy in Cornwall, a short distance from where there had previously been a coastguard station, many of the stations reopened under the auspices of the voluntary National Coastwatch Institution in December 1994. Today there are fifty-eight watch stations around the English and Welsh coast, operated by over 2,600 volunteer watch keepers drawn from all walks of life.

The mission of the National Coastwatch Institution is to assist in the protection and preservation of life at sea and along the UK coastline in support of HM Coastguard. They achieve this by scanning the horizon using state of the art binoculars, Automatic Identification System (AIS), radar, telecoms, internet links, weather instruments, admiralty charts, VHF radios and, of course, the mark 1 human eyeball.

National Coastwatch Institution, Peveril Point
This lookout has been in situ since 1830 and had been manned by the Coastguard since the 1870s, until its closure in 1990. However, by 1995, the NCI lookout was re-established

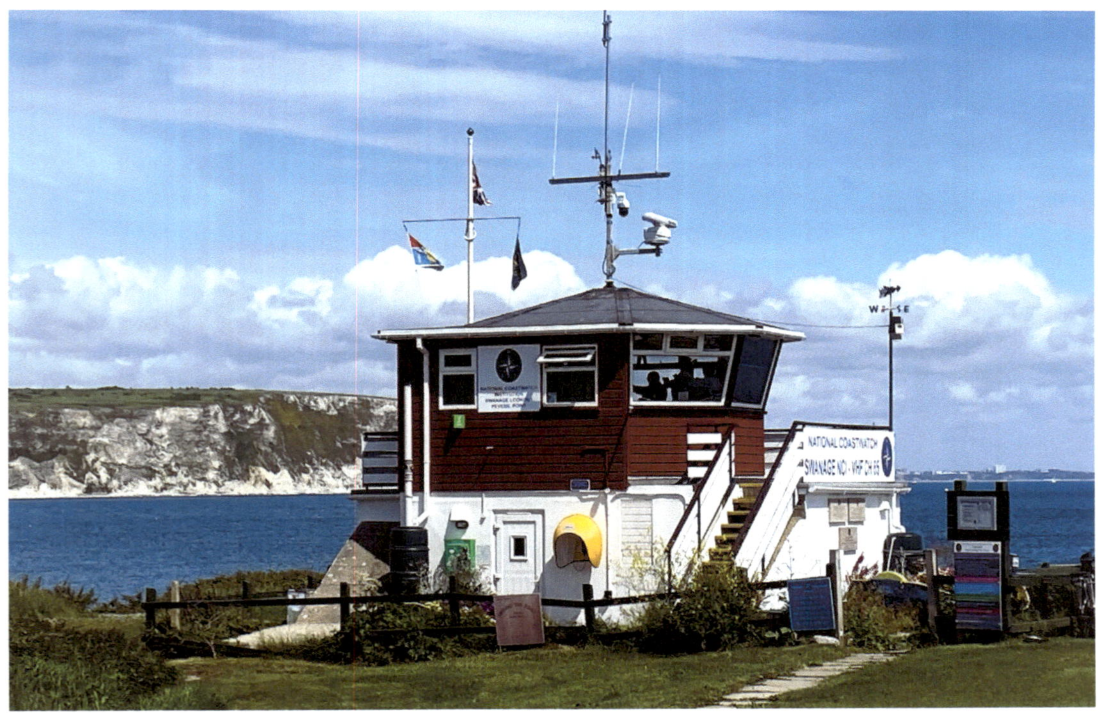

National Coastwatch Institution (NCI), Peveril Point.

and is now manned by over fifty trained volunteers, who between them cover most daylight hours, keeping a watch over one of the busiest stretches of coastline in the UK.

The volunteers here also trained the watchkeepers that went on to reopen the NCI station at St Alban's Head.

National Coastwatch Institution, St Alban's Head

DID YOU KNOW?
On St Aldhelm's Head, the NCI leases the building at a modest rent of one crab per annum if demanded.

The original coastguard station at St Alban's Head was built in 1895 and was replaced with the present building in 1970. It has a commanding view from Portland Bill to St Catherine's Point on the Isle of Wight, allowing the volunteers to keep a watchful eye on the notorious St Alban's Race on either side of the promontory, as well as the Kimeridge Ledges, Weymouth Bay and Anvil Point.

This facility was reopened in 1995 as a substation of NCI Peveril Point, before becoming independent the following year.

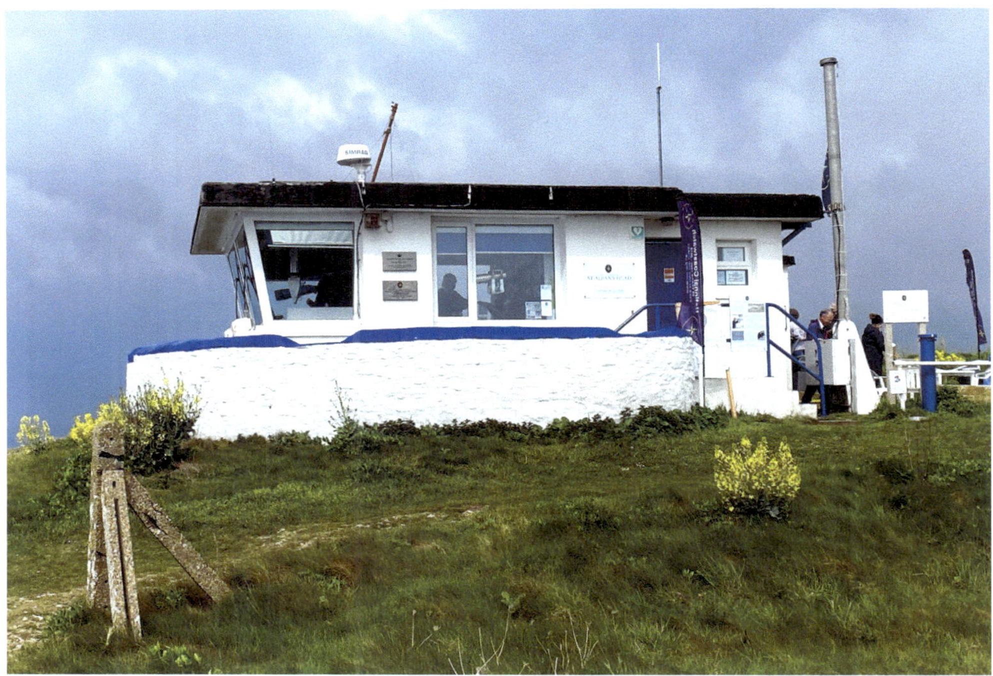

National Coastwatch Institution (NCI), St Alban's Head.

In 2012, the station was awarded the Queen's Golden Jubilee Award for voluntary service.

Coastguard Cliff Rescue Team, Weston, Worth Matravers
In the 1950s the Auxiliary Coastguard Cliff Rescue Team were established inland at Weston, Worth Matravers, and are still in operation today.

Coastguard Cottages
Coastguard cottages feature prominently on many Purbeck coastal sites for instance at Studland, Peveril Point, St Alban's Head and Kimmeridge. They were initially built for the coastguards in the 1800s when the main aim of the coastguard was to prevent smuggling.

Royal National Lifeboat Institution (RNLI), Swanage
In 1875, at the instigation of Charles Robinson and George Burt (see *Wild Wave*), Swanage received its first lifeboat, which was named *Charlie Mary*.

In 2016, the station was rebuilt at its original site close to Swanage Pier and Peveril Point in order to accommodate a Shannon Class all-weather lifeboat, as well as another smaller inshore lifeboat.

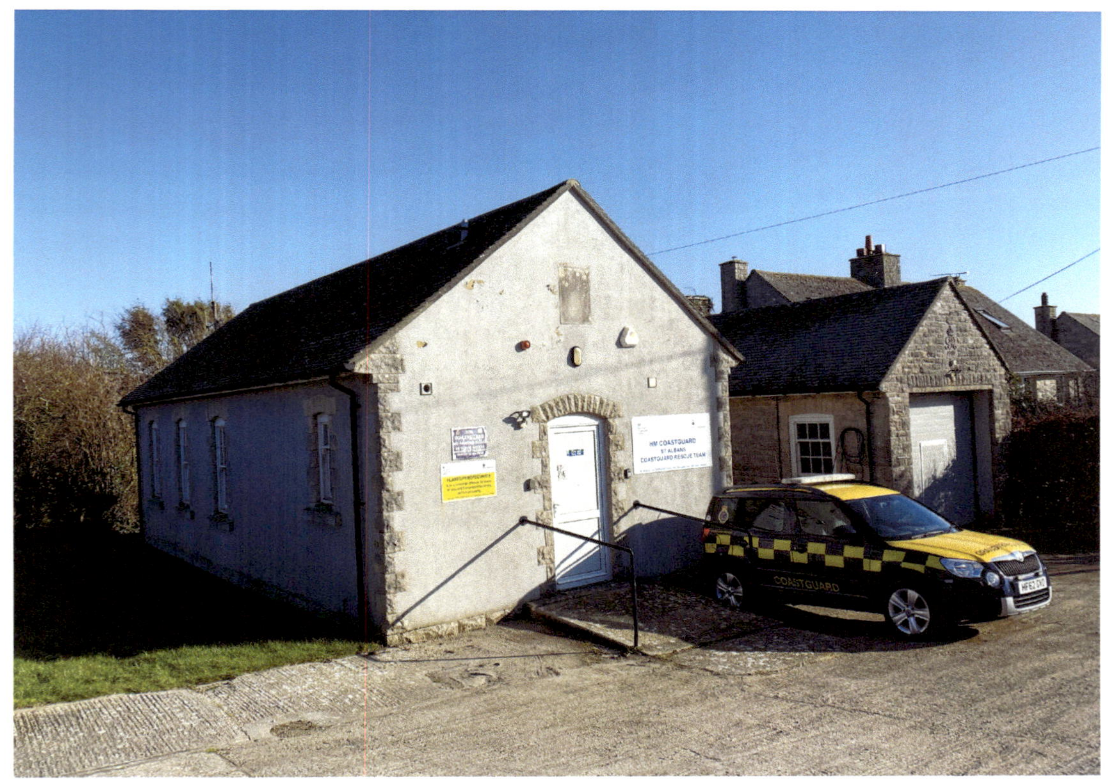

Worth Matravers Coastguard.

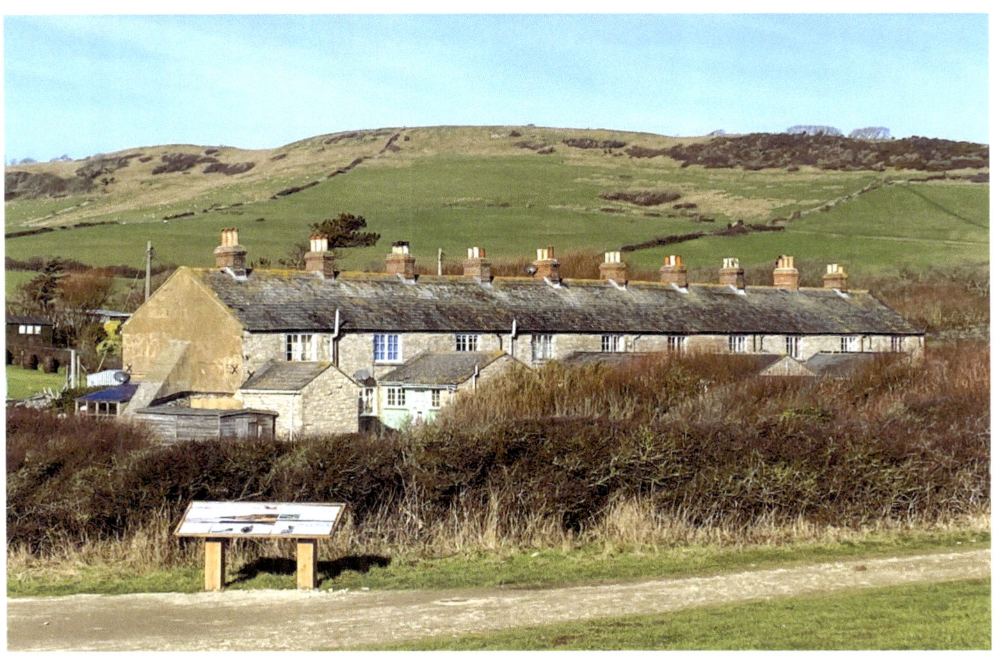

The coastguard cottages on the eastern edge of Kimmeridge Bay were built in 1834 to attempt to put an end to the smuggling that was taking place at Chapman's Pool.

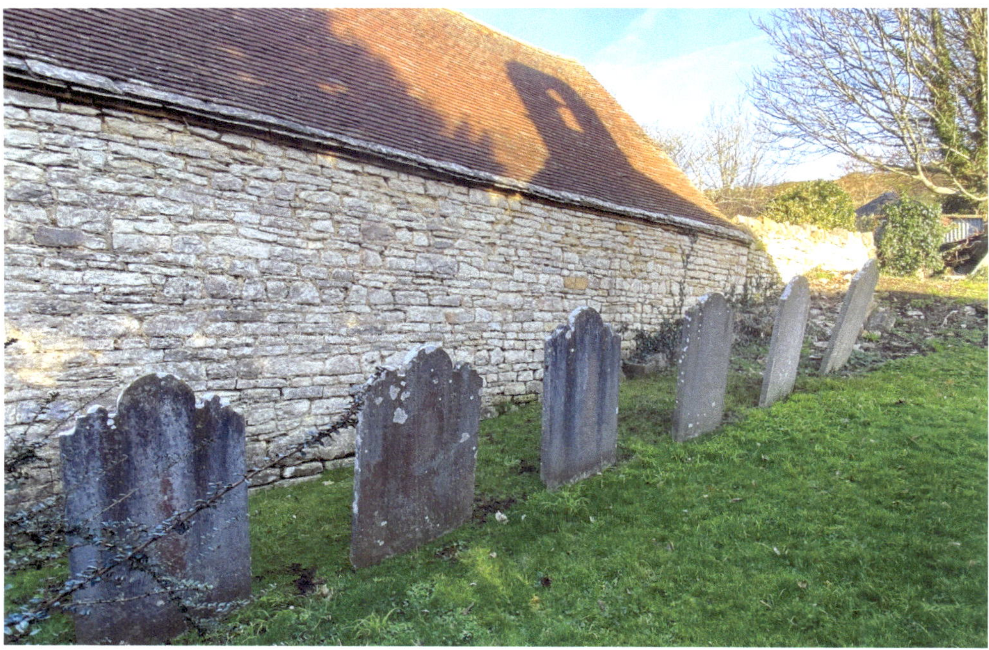

The coastguard graves in the churchyard of St Nicholas' Church, Kimmeridge, are in memory of those who lost their lives in the execution of their duty.

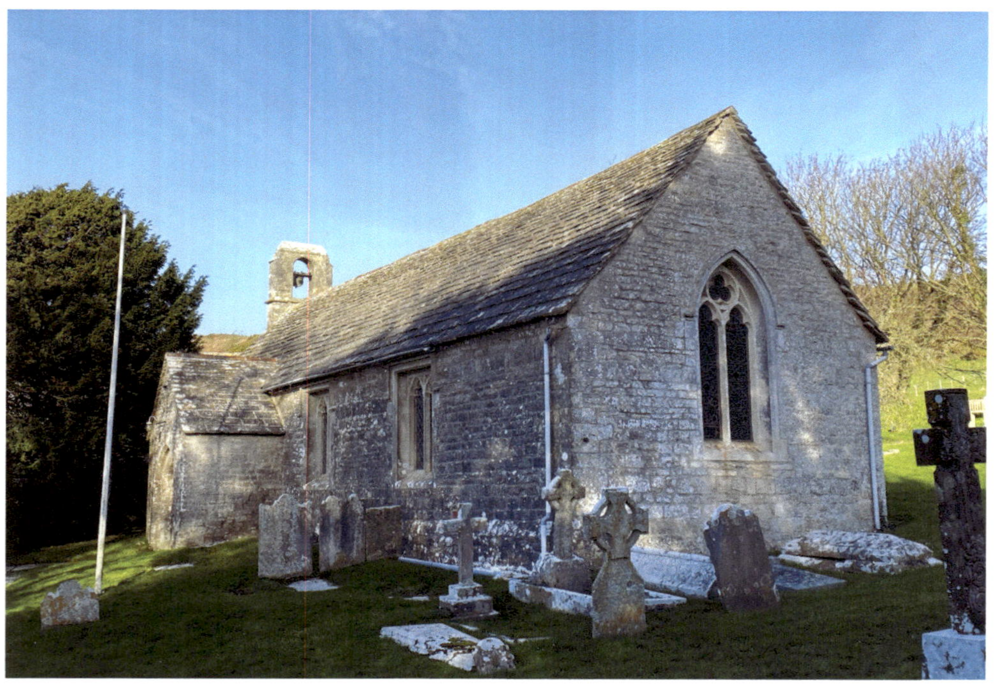

St Nicholas' Church, Kimmeridge.

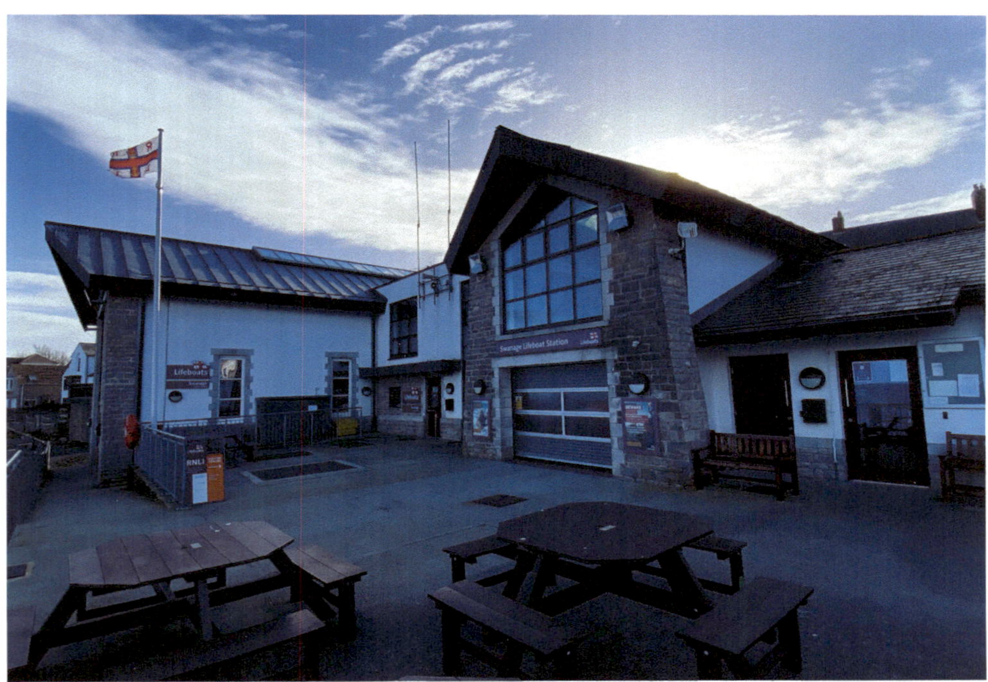

RNLI Station, Swanage.

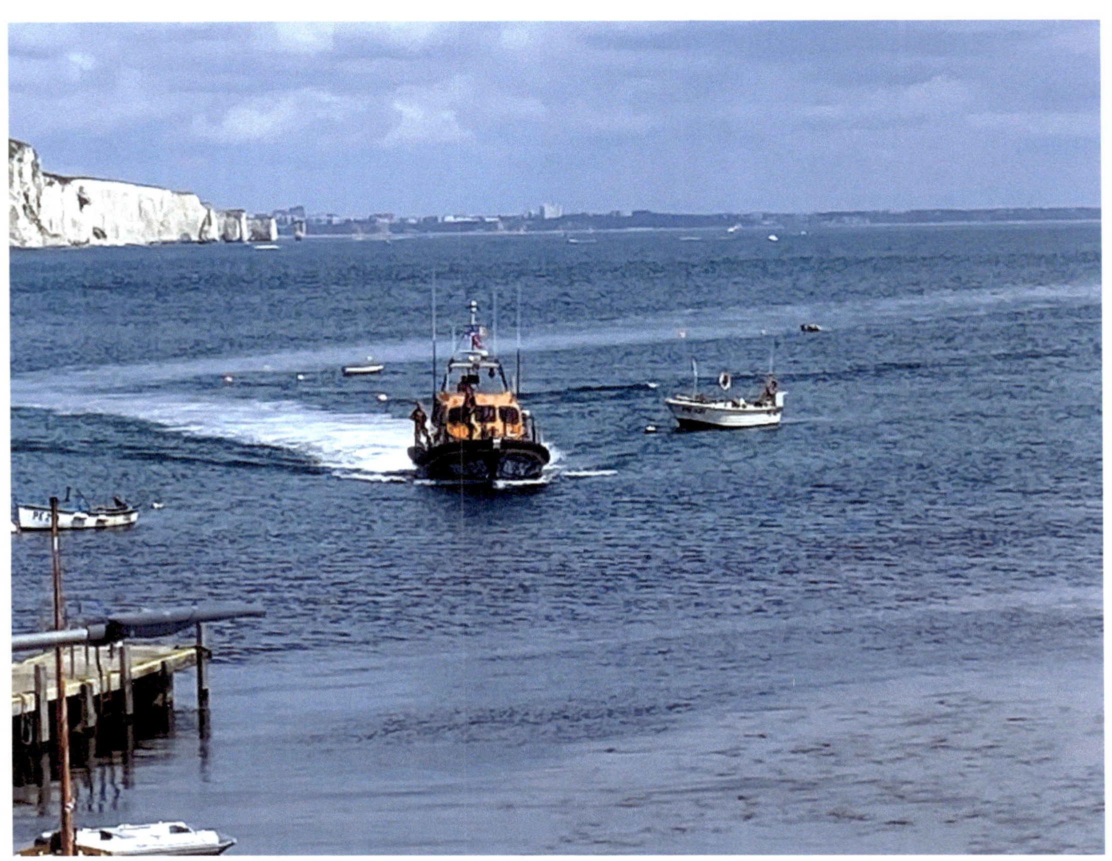

The Swanage lifeboat returning.

Bibliography

Books

Ashley, H., *Dorset Yarns* (Countryside Books, 1999)

Belasco, S., *Dorset from the Sea* (www.veloce.co.uk, 2015)

Cotton, N., *Ordnance Survey Cycle Tours: 24 One-Day Routes in Dorset, Hampshire and Isle of Wight* (Hamlyn, 1993)

Cullingford, A. C. N., *History of Dorset* (Phillimore, 1984)

Dillon, P., *Walking the South West Coast Path* (Cicerone, 2016)

Draper, J., *Dorset: The Complete Guide* (Dovecote Press, 1988)

Hadfield, J., *The Shell Guide to England* (Michael Joseph, 1970)

Heritage of Britain (London: The Reader's Digest Association Ltd, 1985).

Hilliam, D., *The Little Book of Dorset* (History Press, 2010)

Jackson, A., *A–Z of Poole* (Amberley Publishing, 2020)

Jackson, A., *Historic England: Dorset* (Amberley Publishing, 2020)

Jackson, A., *Once Upon a Time in the South West* (Amazon, 2021)

Jackson, A., *Poole Pubs* (Amberley Publishing, 2019)

Jackson, A., *Secret Bournemouth* (Amberley Publishing 2023)

Jurassic Coast Trust, *The Official Guide to the Jurassic Coast* (Jurassic Coast Trust, 2021)

Potts, J., *Phillips Encyclopedia* (Octopus Publishing, 2004)

Power, M., *Pub Walks in Dorset* (Power Publications, 1989)

Sorenson, P., *Stitched Up for the Cup* (Austin Macauley Publishers Ltd, 2021)

Stonehouse, A., 50 walks in Dorset (AA Publishing 2002)

The History of the Kings and Queens of England and Scotland (Wigston: Armadillo Books, 2007)

Townsend, T., *Dorset Smugglers' Pubs* (Pixz Books, 2015)

Townsend, T., *A Guide to Dorset Shipwrecks from the South West Coast Path* (Pixz Books 2020)

Westwood, R., *Fossils and Rocks of the Jurassic Coast* (Inspiring Places Publishing, 2018)

Whaley, P., *West Country History* (Venton, 1977)

Magazines

Active Retirement (Oct 22, p. 12, Issue 1)

Leaflets and Booklets

The Victorian Trail – Dorset Council
History Durlston Country Park National Nature Reserve – Durlston Country Park
Durlston Country Park – Durlston Country Park
Victorian Durlston – Durlston Country Park
National Coastwatch Institution – Swanage
St Nicholas' Church, Studland, Parochial Church Council, St Nicholas, Studland, 2012.
The Church of Lady St Mary Wareham
Welcome to Swanage Pier – Swanage Pier Trust

Information Boards

Diving Club Information Board – Swanage Pier
Fox Inn Corfe Castle
Poole Museum
Square and Compass Museum
Swanage Pier
Wareham Town Museum
Weymouth Museum

Websites

www.ancestorswordpress.com
www.brittainexpress.com
www.calshotdivers.com
www.corfecastle.co.uk
www.divemagazine.com
www.divercol.eclipse.co.uk
www.dorsetancestors.com
www.dorsetand around
www.dorsetaonb.org.uk
www.dorsetcouncil.gov.uk
www.dorsetlife.co.uk
www.dorsetlive.com
www.englishheritage.co.uk
www.historicengland.org.uk
www.historicuk.com
www.livescience.com
www.localhistories.org
www.loquis.com
www.Megalithic.co.uk

www.relevantresearchscotland.co.uk
www.resortdorset.com
www.shorelinesummer2018charmouth.org
www.smithsonianmag.com
www.southwest costpath.org.uk
www.swanage.co.uk
www.Swanagemuseum.org.uk
www.virtualswanage
www.visitdorset.com
www.wessexcoastgeology.sotonac.uk
www.wessexresearch.co.uk